OCR
Revise
Sociology

A2

OCR and Heinemann are working together to provide better support for you

Annemarie O'Dwyer
Anna Lise White
Consultant: Carole Waugh

Official Publisher Partnership

Heinemann is an imprint of Pearson Education Limited, a company incorporated in England and Wales, having its registered office at Edinburgh Gate, Harlow, Essex, CM20 2JE. Registered company number: 872828

www.heinemann.co.uk
Heinemann is a registered trademark of Pearson Education Limited

First published 2009

13 12 11 10 09
10 9 8 7 6 5 4 3 2 1

British Library Cataloguing in Publication Data
A catalogue record for this book is available from the British Library

ISBN 978 0 43546 697 8

Edited by Caroline Compton-McPherson
Typeset by Brian Melville
Cover design by Pearson Education Limited
Cover photo/illustration © istock photo/Les Cunliffe
Printed in the United Kingdom by Henry Ling Limited, at the Dorset Press, Dorchester, DT1 1HD

Every effort has been made to contact copyright holders of material reproduced in this book. Any omissions will be rectified in subsequent printings if notice is given to the publishers.

Acknowledgements
The authors and publisher would like to thank Jane Midgley and Ruth Bradshaw, and the Institute for Public Policy Research (IPPR), for permission to reproduce copyrighted material, pp.107–108.

Thank you to my family for their continued support, and good luck to Richmond-upon-Thames College Sociology students.
Annemarie O'Dwyer

Good luck to all the students at Farnborough Sixth Form College.
Anna White

Contents

Introduction

Well, congratulations for getting to this point! This is where all your hard work starts to pay off. This revision workbook has been produced to facilitate and support you in the run up to your A2 exam(s). Remember, the main purpose of this revision workbook is to recap and revise existing knowledge. It will not replace the notes and knowledge that should have been gained from your attendance at taught sessions at your school or college and the supported reading and note taking that you should have completed while using the core textbook: *OCR Sociology A2, Heinemann, 2009.*

How to use this revision guide

The revision workbook has been produced in conjunction with the core textbook; it is to be used to support and to test your sociological knowledge. The workbook includes all areas of the A2 syllabus: Unit 3 (G673): Power and Control; and Unit 4 (G674): Exploring Social Inequality and Difference. The guide is split between the two units; within each unit there will be a breakdown of the topics. After each unit there will be guidance on exam technique, example questions and exemplar answers, these will be in the Exam Café layout which you should be familiar with from the core textbook.

The two units have been broken down into topics; for example, Unit 3 (G673) includes recap and revise revision activities for each topic: crime and deviance, education, mass media, and power and politics. Unit 4 (G674) includes recap and revise revision activities for the study of gender, class, ethnicity and age, as well as activities on sociological research methods. In both units the breakdown includes: a revision checklist, key concepts, mix and match activity, quick fire quiz, theory identifier activity and applying research studies task. Once you have worked your way through the tasks you can check your answers as indicated, either through the answers appearing upside down at the bottom of the page or by referring to the back of the workbook.

Important note! Try to resist the temptation to look at the answers before you have completed the activities; remember, the only person you will be cheating is yourself. If you use the workbook in the way it has been intended then you will be able to organise and plan your revision with confidence to ensure that you get the best result you can.

How to revise

Recap, Revise, Rewind

Throughout the revision workbook you will come across the words: recap, revise and rewind. They are there to help you signpost each stage of your revision, and you will find the signpost at the top right hand side of the page.

 Recap: these activities will help you recap the important concepts.

 Revise: these activities will help you to revise the essential concepts, studies and theories which you will have covered on your course. Remember, your answer can only be considered sociological if you include sociology!

 Rewind: these activities are related to the exam questions in this book. Remember whenever you see this sign to go back to the exam question, the word 'rewind' is to prompt you to really think about whether you are on track and addressing the question asked.

Exam Café: after each topic there is an Exam Café section; the intention of this section is to get you focused on the actual exam. For each unit you will find an example of a well-written answer along with the examiner's comments, which you need to match to the correct part of the student answer. There are also example questions for you to try yourself. For both units the exam questions can be answered by reference to the material in this revision workbook and the core textbook. Furthermore, if you carry out your own reading/research or make use of the work you have completed in your taught sessions, this is likely to improve the quality of your answers.

Exam skills explanation

Both units G673 and G674 will require you to use the skills of knowledge and understanding (AO1), interpretation and application (AO2a) and analysis and evaluation (AO2b). Each 'part' of each unit's exam questions will require a different amount of each skill. Please take note of how much each part of the question requires of what skill (refer to the Exam Café section in this workbook for each unit to help you with this).

Assessment objective (AO):

- Knowledge and understanding (AO1): the studies, theories, concepts and contemporary examples you have learned throughout your course.

- Interpretation and application (AO2a): how well you interpret the knowledge and apply it to a given question/point.

- Analysis and evaluation (AO2b): judgements, criticisms, appraisals and assessment of sociological knowledge.

One useful technique to practise is that of KIE (Knowledge, Interpretation, Evaluation):

- Do I know this? (K)

- Can I interpret this? (I)

- Can I evaluate this? (E)

And finally …

After all your hard work revising and practising exam questions it is important that once you get into the exam you try to relax and don't panic. Take a deep breath and carefully read all the necessary instructions and the exam question before you begin. Remember, this is the moment that you have been working for all year, so go out there and shine like the sociology star you are!

Revision … Where do I start? What do I do?

There are many different ways of revising and it is important to try out different ways and find out which is the most effective for you. The following stages will help you structure your revision.

Stage one of successful revision:

- Using the revision checklists provided in this book, ensure that you have a complete set of notes for each part of the course. If you find that you are missing any parts then try to obtain these either from your teacher, peers, intranet or make your own notes from the core textbook.

- Go through notes and summarise them into shorter paragraphs or bullet points. Make sure that they cover the points suggested in the revision checklist and include the relevant sociologists, concepts, examples and, if relevant, theories.

Stage two of successful revision:

- Begin your revision by putting your knowledge to the test by completing the revision activities in this book. This will help you to identify any areas of weakness.

- Once you have identified the areas you are less confident with, you could try the following revision techniques to help you remember the information: flash cards (postcard size cards with key concepts, sociologists and theories on them); drawing pictures, charts and diagrams; using Post-it notes around your bedroom with key sociological evidence on them. Also you could try putting notes and reminders on your mobile phone, or making a recording of things you need to remember: you can listen to this on your way to school or college or when you are going to sleep. Make informative posters; this can be particularly useful for remembering theory. Another option could be to colour code each sub-topic; this can act as a mental and visual stimulus.

Stage three of successful revision:

- Start to familiarise yourself with the layout of the exam paper, pay particular attention to the instructive words, for example if you are asked to identify 'ways' make sure you know what you are being asked to do (refer to 'Exam question key words' in this book to help you with instructive words, page 7).

- Refer to the 'Exam Café' sections in this book, and have a go at completing the 'Now try your own' questions. You can use the good examples as guides to help you plan and write your answers.

Moving from AS to A2

Now that you have moved on to the A2 part of the course you will need to demonstrate a strong grasp of the skills required in sociology: knowledge and understanding, interpretation and application and analysis and evaluation. These skills are assessed in exactly the same way as they were at AS but you will need to provide more evidence that you can use such skills competently.

The answers that you write will need to be developed in greater depth and length. For example, for Unit G673 you will need to write two essay style answers in 90 minutes. These answers will need to cover several sides of A4 paper and be structured in formal essay style with an introduction and conclusion. Each essay should refer to different sociological arguments in an evaluative way with reference to a range of theories and research studies. You will find more information on how to tackle each exam question for Units G673 and G674 in the Exam Café section of this book.

Moving from A2 to A*

The A* grade has been introduced in order to identify those candidates who gain exceptionally high marks on the A2 component of the course.

In order to achieve an A* you must gain at least 80 per cent of the possible uniform marks (UMS) for your whole A Level and at least 90 per cent of the possible uniform marks (UMS) for the A2 units added together.

The following guidance will help ensure that you gain maximum marks for each skill to enable you to achieve the A* grade.

AO1

1 Make sure that your answers contain an introduction which sets the scene for the question. This could involve identifying a viewpoint which is mentioned in the question or referring to statistics or evidence to illustrate the view given. You should also define any key concepts in the question in your introductory paragraph.

2 Try to ensure that all points are supported by either a theory, research study or statistical or conceptual evidence.

3 Make sure you quote the source and date of any statistics which you refer to.

4 Try to include contemporary material and examples in your answer, such as recent cases or research which has been in the news.

AO2a

5 Make sure that all points are clearly related to the actual question asked. Try to refer back to the wording of the question at the start of each paragraph.

6 Clearly explain how any contemporary examples relate to the question or the arguments which you are writing about.

7 Try to apply a range of arguments or theories to the question rather than just the most obvious. Think around the question.

AO2b

8 Try to provide an evaluative point in relation to every point, theory or research study which you refer to.

9 Try to counter evaluate – make points which evaluate your evaluative points.

10 Make sure your answers contain a conclusion. It is a good idea to save an evaluative point to include in your conclusion rather than simply summarising what has been said before.

The Exam Café sections of this book provide examples of answers which have followed the A* guidance above.

Exam question key words

The following key words will be useful for you to consider once you have reached stage three of your revision. The exams for Unit G673 and Unit G674 will include questions which will require you to answer in a particular way. The questions may use a number of 'instructive' words such as 'explain', 'outline' and 'assess'. It is very important that you know what these words mean; this will ensure that you address what is being asked of you. Take your time to read through the list of words below and then refer to the Exam Café section of this workbook. Look at how the questions are worded and see if you can recognise which are the 'instructive' words. Also included in the list of words below are key words that you may wish to use in your answers, such as 'patterns', 'trends', 'features', etc.

Outline: means to set out the fundamental points/ views of a particular theory and or statement, ensuring that you identify and describe the key points. For example, if you were asked to 'Outline Weberian views of ethnic inequality' you would ensure that you included key Weberian thinkers such as Rex, Tomlinson and Moore and that you explained their theory on the dual labour market and the 'underclass' theory.

Assess: to evaluate or make a judgement about the extent to which a theory, view or statement is accurate. For example, is the functionalist view that crime and deviance is beneficial to society accurate?

Characteristics: these identify a distinctive point; for example, a characteristic of the 'new working class' would be their 'individualistic' attitude.

Features: these are a noticeable part of something; for example, a feature of the traditional upper class is that they are part of a privileged group and, according to Scott, are an 'invisible' class who operate within high levels of social closure.

Evidence: knowledge on which to base a belief, this can be in the form of a view/theory/statement. Can also mean to provide facts and figures which support a particular standpoint. For example, you could use the statistics from the Social Trends website on the top 1 per cent owning 21 per cent of the wealth in the UK (ONS, 2003) as evidence to support the Marxist notion of social class polarisation between the rich and the poor.

Reasons: these can be opinions, judgements or underlying explanations or causes; for example, traditional Marxists argue that the reason for the existence of inequality in our society is because we live in a capitalist society.

Patterns: these are a set of occurrences (something that takes place) or set of features; for example, according to Van Dijk (1991) there is a pattern to how the media represents ethnic minorities in a negative way.

Trends: refers to something that is heading in a general direction over time or where there is a general tendency to something; one of the recent trends in media ownership is 'transnational ownership'.

Rupert Murdoch is a transnational owner; in 2004 his media company News Corporation reached three-quarters of the globe.

Explanations: these are when you use a statement or theory or fact in order to make something clear and understandable and to make an account of something; for example, you could argue that the official retirement age of 65 years explains why many people see this as the social marker for the beginning of old age.

Theories: these are series of ideas, principles and beliefs which seek to explain the way the social world is from a particular view; for example, feminist theories believe that there will always be inequality for women in society as society is patriarchal (dominated by males).

Illustrate: this is when you make a statement clear by providing examples; for example, if you wanted to use statistics to support the existence of the 'ethnic penalty' you could use the statistical evidence from the Commission on Racial Equality (CRE) on the pay difference between ethnic groups.

Advantages: to emphasise the good qualities or positives of something; for example, one advantage of 'globalisation' is that people have been brought closer together through global media such as the Internet.

Disadvantages: to emphasise the bad or negative, to hinder or put an individual in a less desirable position; it could be argued that during our primary socialisation, how we are shaped into certain norms and values may lead to a more or less desirable position later on in our life time. Bourdieu argues that the 'cultural capital' of middle-class families prepares them better for educational success compared with their working-class counterparts.

Discrimination: unfair treatment of an individual or a group that can be based on prejudice, and can be either intentional or unintentional. It is argued that women experience institutional discrimination in the workplace; this can manifest itself in the form of pay difference between males and females. The London Assembly 2008 found that on average in London men earned more than women; they found a 23 per cent pay gap between males and females.

Unit code and Unit title.

Time: ensure that you note how long the exam is and keep this in mind when you are writing your answers. This will help you to keep on track and not run out of time.

Advanced GCE

SOCIOLOGY

Unit G673: Power and Control

Specimen Paper

G673QP

Additional Materials: Answer Booklet (…pages)

Time: 1 hour 30 mins

INSTRUCTIONS TO CANDIDATES

- Answer any **two** of the following twelve essay questions.
- You may choose 2 questions from the same option **or** 1 question from each of two different options

INFORMATION FOR CANDIDATES

- The number of marks for each question is given in brackets [ ] at the end of each question or part of question.
- The total number of marks for this paper is **100**

ADVICE TO CANDIDATES

- Read each question carefully and make sure you know what you have to do before starting your answer.

SPECIMEN

Read the instructions for candidates carefully. Before you begin ensure that you know what is being asked of you. Pay particular attention to how many questions you are required to answer.

This document consists of **2** printed pages and **1** blank page.

SP (SLM) T12103   © OCR 2007   OCR is an exempt Charity   **[Turn Over**

Answer only two questions from the options you have been taught. Do not be tempted to answer an option you have not been taught, as you simply will not have the sociological knowledge to support your answers.

2

Answer any **two** of the following twelve questions

Option 1

Crime and deviance

1   Outline and assess Marxist explanations of crime.   **[50]**

2   Outline and assess sociological explanations of the role of the media in the social construction of crime.   **[50]**

3   Outline and assess the usefulness of official statistics in measuring crime and deviance.   **[50]**

Pay attention to the instructive words (outline and assess).

Option 2

Education

4   Outline and assess functionalist explanations of the relationship between education and work.   **[50]**

5   Outline and assess the view that it is factors outside the school which affect the educational achievement of different social classes.   **[50]**

6   Outline and assess the view that changes to educational policy since 1988 have resulted in greater equality of opportunity for all students.   **[50]**

Option 3

Mass Media

7   Outline and assess the view that the content of the news is determined by media professionals.**[50]**

8   Outline and assess the usefulness of content analysis as a method of media research.   **[50]**

9   Outline and assess the view that the mass media have a direct effect on their audience.   **[50]**

Option 4

Power and Politics

10 Outline and assess the view that people join new social movements as a search for identity.   **[50]**

11 Outline and assess the view that power is concentrated in the hand of a minority.   **[50]**

12 Outline and assess the Marxist view that political action is a symbol of resistance and rebellion against capitalism.   **[50]**

Paper Total [100]

9

Introduction

Unit code and Unit title.

Time: ensure that you note how long the exam is and keep this in mind when you are writing your answers. This will help you to keep on track and not run out of time.

Advanced GCE

SOCIOLOGY
Unit G674: Exploring social inequality and difference
Specimen Paper

G674QP

Additional Materials: Answer Booklet (…pages)

Time: 2 hours

INSTRUCTIONS TO CANDIDATES

- Answer questions (1) to (2), and **either** Option 1 or Option 2.

INFORMATION FOR CANDIDATES

- The number of marks for each question is given in brackets [ ] at the end of each question or part of question.
- The total number of marks for this paper is **100**

ADVICE TO CANDIDATES

- Read each question carefully and make sure you know what you have to do before starting your answer.

Read the instructions for candidates carefully. Before you begin ensure that you know what is being asked of you. Pay particular attention to how many questions you are required to answer.

Read the source material and answer questions 1 and 2, and then answer either Option 1 3(a) and 3(b) or Option 2 4(a) and 4(b).

EXPLORING SOCIAL INEQUALITY AND DIFFERENCE

Young people today face complex decisions about their future lives, particularly as they leave compulsory education and begin the transition into adulthood. Research by Midgley and Bradshaw entitled 'Should I stay or should I go?' explores the experiences of 16-19 year olds in rural areas as they leave compulsory education. It focuses on the options available to them as they move from education, to training and employment, and sometimes back again. 5

The methodology starts from the belief that the most valuable and powerful insights into the lives of young people are offered by researching the views of young people themselves. The research is located within interpretivism. The research participants were all aged 16-19 and were from 4 different parts of rural England. In each area focus 10 groups were held with the following groups of young people:

- Not in employment, education or training (females, NEET*)

- Not in employment, education or training (males, NEET*)

- In employment (females/males together)

- In education and training (females/males together) 15

Make sure that you pay particular attention to the instructions in bold.

You must answer **both** compulsory questions. Question 1 is instructing you to refer directly to the source provided, as well as ensuring that you use your wider sociological knowledge.

As an A Level unit candidates are encouraged to show an understanding of the links between the nature of sociological thought, the methods of sociological enquiry and the core themes of power, social inequality, socialisation, culture and identity. Candidates are encouraged to think holistically and develop their skills of thinking as a sociologist.

COMPULSORY QUESTIONS

1 Using the item and your own knowledge outline and explain how focus groups may be used in sociological research. **[15]**

2 Outline and assess the claim made by some sociologists that the most valuable and powerful insights into the lives of young people are offered by researching the views of young people themselves. (lines 7-8) **[25]**

Compulsory Questions Total [40]

Then answer either

OPTION 1

3 (a) Outline the evidence that some social groups are marginalised in society. **[20]**

   (b) Assess Marxist explanations of social inequality. **[40]**

Option 1 Total [60]

Or

OPTION 2

4 (a) Outline the evidence that men are disadvantaged in society. **[20]**

   (b) Assess feminist explanations of gender inequality in the workplace. **[40]**

Option 2 Total [60]

Paper Total [100]

You must answer both parts (a) and (b) from either option 1 or 2. You cannot mix and match the options, so read the questions carefully before you attempt to answer them, to ensure you will be able to answer both parts of the option you choose.

Introduction

Crime and deviance

Revision checklist

You are at stage one of the revision process; the list below outlines all the topics and sub-topics which you need to cover in your revision. Take time now to make sure you have everything you need to revise this part of the course. The points referred to below can all be found in the core textbook. Your teacher(s) may also have taught you other sociological research studies, in which case you should also revise these. Tick off the areas once you have revised them and track your progress through the topics.

The definition and measurement of crime and deviance

- Crime (definition and examples) ☐
- Deviance (definition and examples) ☐
- Relativity of crime and deviance (definition and explanation with examples) ☐
- Social construction of crime and deviance (definition and explanation with examples) ☐
- Official statistics (definition, examples, strengths and weaknesses) ☐
- Victim surveys (definition, examples, strengths and weaknesses) ☐
- Self-report studies (definition, examples, strengths and weaknesses) ☐

Trends, patterns and explanations of crime and deviance

- Gender and crime (patterns and trends using statistics) ☐
- Ethnicity and crime (patterns and trends using statistics) ☐
- Social class and crime (patterns and trends using statistics) ☐
- Geographical location and crime (patterns and trends using statistics) ☐
- Age and crime (patterns and trends using statistics) ☐

- Functionalism and crime (research studies, key concepts and evaluation) ☐
- Subcultural theories and crime (research studies, key concepts and evaluation) ☐
- Marxism and crime (research studies, key concepts and evaluation) ☐
- New criminology (research studies, key concepts and evaluation) ☐
- Interactionism and crime (research studies, key concepts and evaluation) ☐
- Left and right realism (research studies, key concepts and evaluation) ☐
- New right and crime (research studies, key concepts and evaluation) ☐
- Feminism and crime (research studies, key concepts and evaluation) ☐

Patterns and explanations of victimisation

- Victims of crime (patterns and trends using statistics) ☐
- Left realism and victimisation (research studies, key concepts and evaluation) ☐
- Feminism and victimisation (research studies, key concepts and evaluation) ☐

The role of agents of social control in the construction of crime and deviance

- Police (explanations and research studies of how they exercise social control) ☐
- Courts (explanations and research studies of how they exercise social control) ☐
- Media (explanations and research studies of how they exercise social control) ☐

Solutions to the problem of crime

Key concepts:

- Crime prevention ☐
- Retributive justice ☐
- Restorative justice ☐
- Incarceration ☐
- Rehabilitation

Left realism (solutions to crime and example of relevant government policy) ☐

Right realism (solutions to crime and example of relevant government policy) ☐

Feminism (solutions to crime and example of relevant government policy) ☐

Key concepts

This recap activity will ensure that you go over those all-important key concepts.
Complete the key concept chart by writing a definition of the concept and, where
possible, include which sociologist uses it. Refer to your core textbook or your
classroom notes.

Key concept	Definitions
Crime	
Deviance	
Official statistics	
Victim surveys	
Self-report studies	
Crime prevention	
Retributive justice	
Restorative justice	
Incarceration	
Rehabilitiation	
Moral panic	
Deviancy amplification	

Mix and match

The purpose of this exercise is to test your knowledge of key pieces of sociological research within the topic of crime and deviance. You will need to match the explanation of the research with the name of the sociologist. Each sociologist is numbered and the explanation of study is lettered. Match the correct explanation with the sociologist by writing the correct letter in the blank box provided. Then check at the bottom of the page to see if you have matched the two correctly.

Sociologist

1 Hebdige ☐

2 Adler ☐

3 Merton ☐

4 Newburn ☐

5 Carrabine ☐

6 Gilroy ☐

7 Atkinson ☐

Research/theory

A
Crime and deviance are caused by the inability of some members of society to achieve society's shared goals legitimately.

B
It will never be clear if someone has actually committed suicide. All we know is that the death has been defined as a suicide.

C
Crime and deviance by the working classes are a form of resistance and rebellion against capitalist society.

D
There has been an increase in the number of crimes committed by women and this is a result of the impact of feminism.

E
Ethnic minority crime is a reaction to racism and part of a political struggle against the white oppressor.

F
There is a hierarchy of victimisation – some victims enjoy a higher status than others.

G
There has been a decline in rape crisis centres but an increase in the number of reported rapes.

Answers: 1.C, 2.D, 3.A, 4.G, 5.F, 6.E, 7.B

Check your knowledge quick fire quiz

This multiple choice quiz will test your knowledge of crime and deviance. Each question will be worth a number of points; the points are indicated at the end of the question. The more points a question is worth, the more difficult it is: the top mark questions reflect whether you have read your core textbook thoroughly. Once you have ticked the answer you believe to be correct, add up your score to reveal whether you are a crime and deviance expert!

1 *Which source of official statistics on crime involves asking people if they have been victims of crime?* **(2 points)**

a) ☐ The British Crime Survey

b) ☐ Delinquent Development Survey

c) ☐ Youth Lifestyles Survey

2 *The following statement is a criticism of which sociological theory? 'The theory does not explain crimes which are not caused by material deprivation or political rebellion.'* **(3 points)**

a) ☐ Functionalism

b) ☐ Feminism

c) ☐ Marxism

3 *Which of the following terms is used to describe the way in which the police do not record crimes which they think they will be unable to solve?* **(2 points)**

a) ☐ Coughing

b) ☐ Cuffing

c) ☐ Plea bargaining

4 *According to the Youth Justice Board's report in 2008, how many crimes were committed by girls aged between 10 and 17?* **(4 points)**

a) ☐ 59,236

b) ☐ 29,536

c) ☐ 95,236

5 *Which of the following is not one of the focal concerns of the working class identified by Miller?* **(3 points)**

a) ☐ Toughness

b) ☐ Excitement

c) ☐ Fighting

6 *Who argues that Asian crime has increased in recent years due to Asian males moving outside of their cultural group in a way that their parents did not?* **(3 points)**

a) ☐ Sewell

b) ☐ Desai

c) ☐ Gilroy

7 *Which government report was published in response to the murder of Stephen Lawrence and found the police to be institutionally racist?* **(3 points)**

a) ☐ The Macpherson Report

b) ☐ The McDonald Report

c) ☐ The BPS Report

Possible 20 points

17–20 Well done! You are a crime and deviance expert!

12–16 It's official: you are becoming a 'sociology star'!

7–11 Looks like you might be avoiding the more difficult questions – get back to reading that textbook!

0–6 Oh dear, you're not going to win any 'sociology student of the year' prizes!

Answers: 1.a, 2.c, 3.b, 4.a, 5.c, 6.b, 7.a

Theory identifier

The statements below reflect the viewpoints of one of the following theories: functionalism, subcultural theory, Marxism, new criminology, interactionism, left realism, new right or feminism. Identify which theory goes with which statement by writing in the space above the statement.

1 _____

Labelling people as deviant can make them become more deviant.

2 _____

Crime and deviance provide employment. This makes a significant contribution to the economy.

3 _____

Crime is a response to the generosity of the welfare state which makes people lazy and gives them no incentive to work. This in turn means they grow up with little discipline and are more likely to commit crime.

4 _____

Crime is a result of poverty and is caused by the capitalist system. People steal because they do not have enough money as the wages paid in a capitalist economy are too low.

5 _____

Individuals choose to commit crimes; they are not just puppets of the economy. For example, some crimes may have political rather than economic motives.

6 _____

Young working-class people may commit crime as a way of rebelling against the norms and values of capitalist society.

7 _____

Women are less likely to commit crime because they have more controls placed on their behaviour.

8 _____

Working-class males possess a distinctive subculture. This subculture possesses its own values which may lead its members to commit crimes. For example, values such as toughness and autonomy.

9 _____

In analysing crime and deviance we should consider four elements: the state, the offender, society and the victim.

Crime and deviance

Answers: 1. interactionism, 2. functionalism, 3. new right, 4. Marxism, 5. new criminology, 6. Marxism, 7. feminism, 8. subcultural theory 9. left realism

Applying research studies task

The following is a list of some of the key concepts you may need to refer to when answering questions on the crime and deviance unit. Fill in the blank column with details of a sociologist and their research which could be used to illustrate each concept. The first one is done for you. Answers can be found at the back of the book.

Key concept	Sociologist/research
Social order	Durkheim (1938) argued that societies need social order. Crime and deviance pose a threat to social order and should therefore be challenged and controlled through the legal system.
Anomie	
Meritocracy	
Cultural deprivation	
Material deprivation	
Chivalry thesis	
Corporate crime	
Folk devils	
Broken windows	

ExamCafé

Power and control: crime and deviance

The skills you gained at AS level must also be applied to your A2 exam responses. It is very important that you not only refresh your memory of the necessary skills but that you are also aware of how many marks you could potentially be awarded for each skill. These marks are summarised below:

◆ AO1 Knowledge and understanding = 23 marks
◆ AO2a Interpretation and application = 10 marks
◆ AO2b Analysis and evaluation = 17 marks
Total marks = 50

Exam answer-based activity

The answer below is an example of a well-written response to a G673 crime and deviance question. Your task is to match the examiner's comments listed at the bottom with the numbers listed in the body of the exam answer. You must correctly match the lettered examiner comments with the numbered points. You can then check at the bottom of the page to see if you have matched them correctly. The purpose of this activity is to give you an awareness of the key points which are required to answer this question and of where the skills of AO1, AO2a and AO2b are being used.

Outline and assess the usefulness of official statistics in measuring crime and deviance. (50 marks)

Student answer

Each year the police and other law enforcement agencies collect information on crime that has been committed and it is published by the Home Office. The results that are collected and collated by the law enforcement agencies are known as official crime statistics (OCS). Official crime statistics are collected in order to establish the volume of crime over a certain period of time, find patterns and trends in crime statistics, and the official crime statistics also produce information of the characteristics of people that commit crime in relation to age, gender, social class and ethnicity. Official statistics on crime are also supplemented by other approaches to measuring crime such as self-report studies and victim studies. **1** ☐

The Home Office looks into the number of crimes committed each year, and makes evaluations. From the official crime statistics, it has been found that the crimes which occur most frequently are theft and handling stolen goods. The average age of a criminal in 1998 was 18, compared with 14 years of age in the 1950s, which does show a rise over time. Official statistics published by the Home Office in 2006 show that 80 per cent of offenders were male. **2** ☐

Although the official crime statistics give information on what types of crime have been committed and who by, they have had a number of criticisms and questions about their validity and reliability. Pilkington suggested that official crime statistics were unreliable for a number of reasons. Firstly, they do not include summary offences, i.e. crimes that have only been tried in Magistrates Courts, neither do they take into account crimes that are to do with the Inland Revenue, such as white-collar and corporate crimes, which are actually a rising problem, as I will later discuss. Other reasons this collection and method of measuring crime has been questioned and criticised is because of the 'dark figure of crime'. There are a great number of crimes that are not reported to the police for a number of reasons. **3** ☐

People may be reluctant to report a crime to the police if they feel the matter is too trivial, such as a minor assault or vandalism; They may feel embarrassed about reporting certain incidents to the police, such as child abuse, or incidents that involve some kind of sexual abuse. Also, people may not realise they have been a victim of crime, this applies to people who have been a victim of some form of white-collar crime, or even people may feel the police won't deal with their matter efficiently.

All these factors make people reluctant to report crimes to the police and this affects the validity of this method of measurement of crime. A true and accurate picture of crime is not being portrayed. The OCS are problematic for other reasons. Over 40 per cent of reported crimes are not recorded by the police. Again, this seriously affects their validity. Barclay suggests that only around 2 per cent of all crimes reported do actually go on to be tried in courts. **4** ☐

There are a number of reasons why police may choose to ignore and not record reported incidents. This could depend on the seriousness of the incident; if the incident is trivial they may choose to ignore the report. Another factor which affects police recording of crime could be the social class of the person reporting. For example, if someone of a very low social status reported an offence the police may not take them seriously, i.e. homeless people, and again choose not to record the crime. This idea is backed by interactionist sociologist Becker, who claims that enforcement of the law is affected by the interpretation and selection of the police. Becker suggests that criminal and deviant people are those who have been labelled as such and often these labels are based on stereotypes. However, interactionists are criticised for being too deterministic as not everyone will accept labels given to them.

As well as the non-reporting and non-recording of crime, there are various other suggestions by sociologists that OCS may not be useful. Holdaway argues that OCS are socially constructed, i.e. the end outcome of a number of interactions. He suggests the police look out for two types of characters: the 'typically criminal' or the 'respectable'. It has been proven by sociologists that when police choose to stop and search people they go for certain indicators, such as dress, speech, ethnicity, etc. This police stereotyping could reflect the over-representation of Afro-Caribbeans in the OCS; despite the fact that they make up only 2.3 per cent of the population, they make up a greater percentage of stop and searches, arrests and form a greater proportion of the prison population. It has been argued that this is a result of institutional racism with the police targeting this group due to stereotypes held. These stereotypes may be reinforced by the media. For example, Hall argues that in the 1970s the media moral panic about 'mugging' led to a high number of young black males being targeted by the police under the 'Sus law'. There is also more recent evidence of this with the moral panic about knife crime leading to the police targeting this group using the powers of 'stop and account' and 'stop and search'. Phillips and Bowling argue that ethnic neighbourhoods are over policed and the police use military-style methods. Self-report studies conducted by the Home Office (2004) show that black and white people commit similar amounts of crime. However, there may be ethnic differences which affect how truthful people are when completing self-report surveys. **5** ☐

Policing practices could also reflect the fact that there is also an over-representation of working-class males, and an under-representation of females in the OCS. Flood-Page points out that self-report studies show that women commit more crime than is illustrated by the OCS. The chivalry thesis proposes that this is because they are treated more leniently by police and courts who view them as vulnerable and in need of protection. However, there is evidence that the number of crimes committed by females has increased, as has the use of custodial sentences for women.

It is clear that police practices have a negative impact on the OCS method of measuring crime, but other law enforcement agencies and agents of social control add to this too. Hood's study into 3,300 cases at West Midlands Crown Court found that black defendants had a 17 per cent higher chance of being convicted than their white counterparts. This evidence could show stereotypical and racist opinions and views on behalf of the official members of Court.

Hood also suggested that the OCS may be problematic because of the over-representation of working-class males and Afro-Caribbeans. Hood did another study and found that around 80 per cent of magistrates came from higher social classes 1+2; this could lead to the magistrates giving harsher, more frequent sentences to working-class and Afro-Caribbean males, which again will affect the validity of the official crime statistics.

Griffiths also did a study into the background of judges, and again found that a high majority of judges were from upper-middle-class social backgrounds and many attended top education areas such as Oxford. This could lead to bias and discrimination by the judges towards the defendants that came before them, due to their opposing backgrounds.

Hood also argued that there was an under-representation of working-class males and also members of certain ethnic groups that appeared on the magistrates bench; again this could have an impact on the number of people that get convicted, alongside their social status and ethnicity, etc. Phenomenologists argue that when in court, individuals can present an image of themselves that will affect their chance of being prosecuted and that they can negotiate their way out of the criminal justice system.

Traditional Marxists such as Gordon have been highly critical of the OCS as although working-class people and crimes dominate the statistics, they do not take into account middle-class, capitalist crimes such as white-collar crimes. Marxists believe that these are not taken into account because law enforcement agencies aim to protect the ruling classes, and that is the reason there is greater emphasis on working-class crimes rather than these white-collar or corporate crimes. **6** ☐ Box argues that law enforcement agencies do aim to protect the ruling classes, and aim to portray the 'problem population' as being working class and Afro-Caribbean. He concludes that the OCS as a method of measuring crime is ideological. However, left realists, such as Jock and Young, argue that although the OCS may be inaccurate due to the fact that there may be over-policing of certain areas, they are not 100 per cent inaccurate; in their Islington Crime Survey they found that in inner cities the most common type of offenders were the working class and also Afro-Caribbeans.

In order to overcome some of the weaknesses of OCS, alternative methods of measuring crime have been introduced. These include victimisation studies and self-report studies. The most prominent example of a victim study is the British Crime Survey (BCS). It collects information on 15,000 households over the UK to make it as representative as possible. It is hoped the survey will collect information on crimes which have not been reported to the police. However, this method of collecting and measuring crime is also problematic. Firstly, it depends upon people's memory, which could be faulty or biased, and also, even though the participant remains anonymous, still people do not admit to being a victim of a sexual offence. This was seen as highly unrealistic and so was criticised by left realists Jock and Young. They criticised the method of measuring crime due to their methodology. They believed a questionnaire was not a good method as people will not answer honestly and openly. Jock and Young did their own study, the Islington Crime Survey, in which they used sympathetic interviewers in order to uncover statistics about sensitive issues such as rape and domestic violence. They concluded that people's fear of crime was realistic; therefore challenging the results of BCS results and also that an inner-city dweller was not an 'average' person; they had in fact a higher chance of being a victim of crime.

Self-report studies usually involve questionnaires being sent out to a cross section of the population asking which offences they have committed in the previous twelve months. These surveys are often directed at younger members of the population, an example being the Youth Lifestyles Survey. These surveys aim to gather information on crimes which may not have been detected or reported to the police. However, there also problems with these which may affect their usefulness. Problems may occur with representativeness. There is a low response rate and it may be that only those who have not committed crimes return them. They would not be sent to the homeless or those who are in prison already and may have committed other crimes. A major problem is that people may lie. This would reduce the validity of this method.

It is evident that all methods of measuring crime are problematic and raise issues about validity, reliability and representativeness. However, this does not mean that they are not useful. Official statistics give us a national picture of crime and do not involve any additional costs in their collation / production; without these the figure of crime which we see would be much 'darker' than it currently is. 7 ☐

Examiner comments

a) Effective use of statistics to set the scene of the question. These are effectively sourced with the date and publisher. (AO1)

b) Effective application of different theoretical perspectives such as Marxism and phenomenology. (AO2a)

c) Good use of key concepts and phrases such as 'dark figure of crime'. (AO1)

d) New paragraphs are well linked back to the question which will help the candidate capitalise on interpretation and application (AO2a) marks.

e) A well-written introduction which clearly explains what official statistics are. (AO1)

f) A clear conclusion which refers back to the exact wording of the question and draws the answer to a firm end. (AO2a)

g) Points are clearly evaluated, especially at the end of key paragraphs. (AO2b)

Answers: 1.e, 2.a, 3.c, 4.d, 5.g, 6.b, 7.f.

Now try your own

Now try to write answers to the questions below. It is a good idea to try writing these answers under timed conditions. You should spend 45 minutes writing each answer.

- Outline and assess functionalist explanations of crime. (50 marks)
- Outline and assess sociological explanations of the relationship between gender and crime. (50 marks)
- Outline and assess the usefulness of self-report studies in measuring crime. (50 marks)

Education

Revision checklist

You are at stage one of the revision process; the list below outlines all the topics and sub-topics which you need to cover in your revision. Take time now to make sure you have everything you need to revise this part of the course. The points referred to below can all be found in the core textbook. Your teacher(s) may also have taught you other sociological research studies, in which case you should also revise these. Tick off the areas once you have revised them and track your progress through the topics.

The structure and organisation of the education system
Key concepts:
- Formal curriculum ☐
- Hidden curriculum ☐
- Equality of opportunity ☐
- Equality of outcome ☐
- Competition ☐
- Marketisation ☐
- Parentocracy ☐

Examples and explanations of the main educational policies from 1988 to the present day ☐

The role and function of education in society
- Functionalism and education (research studies, concepts and evaluation) ☐
- Marxism and education (research studies, concepts and evaluation) ☐
- Social democratic views on education (research studies, concepts and evaluation) ☐
- Interactionism and education (research studies, concepts and evaluation) ☐
- New right views on education (research studies, concepts and evaluation) ☐

Differential educational achievement
Patterns and trends:
- Social class and education (patterns and trends using statistics) ☐

- Ethnicity and education (patterns and trends using statistics) ☐
- Gender and education (patterns and trends using statistics) ☐

Theoretical explanations:
- Cultural factors (research studies, concepts and evaluation) ☐
- Material factors (research studies, concepts and evaluation) ☐
- Processes within the school (research studies, concepts and evaluation) ☐
- Functionalism (research studies, concepts and evaluation) ☐
- Marxism (research studies, concepts and evaluation) ☐
- Interactionism (research studies, concepts and evaluation) ☐
- Social democratic (research studies, concepts and evaluation) ☐
- Feminism (research studies, concepts and evaluation) ☐
- New right (research studies, concepts and evaluation) ☐

The interrelationship between class, gender and ethnicity (research studies, concepts and evaluation) ☐

The relationship between education and the economy

Examples and explanation of different types of vocational and work-based training ☐

Theoretical explanations of the relationship between education and work:

- Functionalism (research studies, concepts and evaluation) ☐
- Marxism (research studies, concepts and evaluation) ☐
- New right (research studies, concepts and evaluation) ☐
- Liberal / social democratic (research studies, concepts and evaluation) ☐
- Feminism (research studies, concepts and evaluation) ☐

Education and social policy

Examples and explanation of government policies from 1988 to the present day including:

- The Education Reform Act (1988) ☐
- Excellence in Schools (1997) ☐
- The New Deal (1998) ☐
- Widening Participation (2003) ☐

Theoretical explanations:

- New right (explanation and evaluation) ☐
- New Labour (explanation and evaluation) ☐

Key concepts

This recap activity will ensure that you go over those all-important key concepts. Complete the key concept chart by writing a definition of the concept and, where possible, include which sociologist uses it. Refer to your core textbook or your classroom notes.

Key concepts	Definitions
Formal curriculum	
Hidden curriculum	
Equality of opportunity	
Equality of outcome	
Competition	
Marketisation	
Parentocracy	
Vocational education	
Work-based training	

Mix and match

The purpose of this exercise is to test your knowledge of key pieces of sociological research within the topic of education. You will need to match the explanation of the research with the name of the sociologist. Each sociologist is numbered and the explanation of study is lettered. Match the correct explanation with the sociologist by writing the correct letter in the blank box provided. Then check at the bottom of the page to see if you have matched the two correctly.

Sociologist

1 Durkheim	☐
2 Coard	☐
3 Sewell	☐
4 Smith and Noble	☐
5 Machin and Vignoles	☐
6 Hargreaves	☐
7 Sue Sharpe	☐

Research/theory

A
Poverty means that children and their parents are unable to afford uniform, trips and things like computers.

B
A key function of education is the creation of a skilled workforce. This is because modern societies require workers who can do complex tasks.

C
EMA (Education Maintenance Allowance) has been positive and has increased disadvantaged students' participation in further education.

D
The school curriculum is ethnocentric. It is based on one cultural viewpoint and ignores others. White history and white literature dominate the curriculum.

E
Afro-Caribbean males underachieve in education because they have a peer group culture which follows an aggressive form of masculinity and is anti-school.

F
Girls' priorities changed between 1976 and 1994. In 1976 girls were interested in marriage and children but in 1994 they wanted jobs and careers.

G
Labelling can have a negative effect on pupils. Those who are placed in the bottom streams of schools often become anti-school and form deviant subcultures.

Check your knowledge quick fire quiz

This multiple choice quiz will test your knowledge of education. Each question will be worth a number of points; the points are indicated at the end of the question. The more points a question is worth, the more difficult it is: the top mark questions reflect whether you have read your core textbook thoroughly. Once you have ticked the answer you believe to be correct, add up your score to reveal whether you are an education expert!

1 *Which piece of education legislation included the introduction of the national curriculum?* **(2 points)**

    a) ☐ 1988 Education Reform Act
    b) ☐ 1944 Education Act
    c) ☐ The New Deal

2 *The following statement is a criticism of which sociological theory? 'The theory concentrates too much on class inequalities in education. It says little about inequalities related to gender and ethnicity.'*
(3 points)

    a) ☐ Functionalism
    b) ☐ Feminism
    c) ☐ Marxism

3 *Which of the following is not a language code identified by Basil Bernstein?* **(2 points)**

    a) ☐ Restricted
    b) ☐ Immediate
    c) ☐ Elaborate

4 *How many women gained university places in autumn 2006?* **(4 points)**

    a) ☐ 210,000
    b) ☐ 102,000
    c) ☐ 220,000

5 *Which of the following is not a subject that girls commonly choose at A Level?* **(3 points)**

    a) ☐ Sociology
    b) ☐ Psychology
    c) ☐ Physics

6 *Who conducted the research on working-class males' experience of education, titled 'Learning to labour: why working-class kids get working-class jobs'?* **(3 points)**

    a) ☐ Tony Sewell
    b) ☐ William Labov
    c) ☐ Paul Willis

7 *Which piece of legislation ensured that regardless of gender, ethnicity or social class, all students up to GCSE level were offered the same compulsory subjects?* **(3 points)**

    a) ☐ The Education Act 1944
    b) ☐ The Education Reform Act 1988
    c) ☐ Curriculum 2000

Possible 20 points

17–20 Well done! You are an education expert!
12–16 It's official: you are becoming a 'sociology star'!
7–11 Looks like you might be avoiding the more difficult questions – get back to reading that textbook!
0–6 Oh dear, you're not going to win any 'sociology student of the year' prizes!

Unit 3: Power and control

Answers: 1.a, 2.c, 3.b, 4.a, 5.c, 6.c, 7.b

Theory identifier

The statements below reflect the viewpoints of one of the following theories: functionalism, Marxism, interactionism, social democratic, feminism or new right. Identify which theory goes with which statement by writing in the space above the statement.

1 _____

It is possible to work within capitalism to provide a fairer education system. The comprehensive education system can provide this and help to create equal opportunities for all classes.

2 _____

Sociologists should be concerned with the small scale interactions within schools rather than the education system as a whole.

3 _____

Education is a key institution in the process of secondary socialisation. It teaches society's shared norms and values.

4 _____

Education should be consumer led and operate according to the principles of a free market economy. Parents should have the power to choose and influence appropriate and effective education.

5 _____

Education has a close correspondence to work. Values that are taught in schools through the hidden curriculum, such as respect for authority and obedience, help to create workers who will be easily exploited.

6 _____

The higher classes have an advantage in the education system because they possess cultural capital.

7 _____

Feminism has played a part in improving the educational achievement of females.

8 _____

The education system should teach pupils the skills and qualifications which are needed by the economy. Vocational education is an important element of education which benefits both individuals and society.

9 _____

Vocational education simply trains workers for exploitation and teaches the skills needed for low paid, low skilled employment.

29

Education

Answers: 1. social democratic, 2. interactionism, 3. functionalism 4. new right, 5. Marxism, 6. Marxism, 7. feminism, 8. functionalism, 9. Marxism

Applying research studies task

The following is a list of some of the key concepts you may need to refer to when answering questions on the education unit. Fill in the spaces in the adjacent column with details of a sociologist and their research which could be used to illustrate each concept. The first one is done for you. Answers can be found at the back of the book.

Key concepts	Sociologist/research
Value consensus	Parsons (1961) argues that schools have a key role in teaching society's norms and values. Schools teach values such as the importance of achievement and equal opportunity, and this leads to a consensus in society.
Role allocation	
Cultural capital	
Self-fulfilling prophecy	
Immediate gratification	
Elaborated and restricted language codes	
Material deprivation	
Anti-school subcultures	
Bedroom culture	
Institutional racism	
Cheap labour	
Knowledge economy	
Personalisation	
EMA	

ExamCafé

Power and control: education

The skills you have gained at AS level must also be applied to your A2 exam responses. It is very important that you not only refresh your memory of the necessary skills but that you are also aware of how many marks you could potentially be awarded for each skill. These marks are summarised below:

◆ AO1 Knowledge and understanding = 23 marks
◆ AO2a Interpretation and application = 10 marks
◆ AO2b Analysis and evaluation = 17 marks

Total marks = 50

Exam answer-based activity

The answer below is an example of a well-written response to a G673 education question. Your task is to match the examiner's comments listed at the bottom with the numbers listed in the body of the exam answer. You must correctly match the lettered examiner comments with the numbered points. You can then check at the bottom of the page to see if you have matched them correctly. The purpose of this activity is to give you an awareness of the key points which are required to answer this question and of where the skills of AO1, AO2a and AO2b are being used.

> Outline and assess sociological explanations of gender differences in educational achievement. (50 marks)   rewind

Student answer

The main gender difference in educational achievement is that males underachieve in comparison with girls. This is supported by statistical evidence from the DfES (2005/06) which shows that 64 per cent of girls achieved five GCSEs grades A*-C compared with 54 per cent of boys. Research also shows that gender differences also occur in the early years of education. Wragg found that the language development of girls was ahead of boys at ages 3-4 and that at ages 5-11 girls were ahead of boys by 5/6 points in standard reading tests. **1** ☐

The first main explanation for male underachievement is that the education system disadvantages boys. The interactionist approach looks at small-scale interactions and experiences within the school and suggests that teachers have lower expectations of boys' ability. Mitsos and Browne found that teachers are more lenient towards boys and give them more leeway with deadlines and expect lower standards of work than girls. This causes boys to underachieve because they are not pushed to fulfil their potential. They also found that boys are more likely to misbehave in lessons and get sent out, causing them to miss academic time. Furthermore, boys are more likely to be excluded from school, with 80 per cent of permanently excluded pupils being male.

Abraham (1986) also found evidence of labelling in education. He carried out research in a co-educational comprehensive school and asked teachers to describe a 'typical girl' and a 'typical boy'. Typical boys were described as mischievous, troublemakers and flirty, while typical girls were described as neat, quiet and accepting of authority. Boys were expected to be badly behaved and received more bad behaviour notes and letters about missed assignments than girls. However, Abraham's own research found that girls and boys were equally willing to complete homework. He found that the students were more likely to be judged upon what teachers expected their behaviour to be than what it was actually like; boys were perceived as being more badly behaved and so were punished more; while girls were perceived as being better behaved and so were believed to be.

This is an example of how the labelling of boys can inhibit their educational achievement, as they will not be treated as being as capable as girls are, which may lead to a self-fulfilling prophecy. However, as research by interactionist sociologists tends to use qualitative methods of research on small samples, this poses problems with the representativeness of the findings. **2** ☐

Another explanation that suggests that the education system disadvantages boys and causes male underachievement is the biological explanation. Moir suggests that boys and girls naturally learn in different ways and have different abilities and interests. However, the education system teaches them in the same way and so he suggests that this is why boys underachieve, especially in subjects like English and languages. He says that these differences are made worse by 'girl-friendly' schools which teach boys in a feminine way. He suggests that the classroom has experienced feminisation, which means that boys are taught in a girl-friendly manner such as emphasising communication. He suggests that boys find the female classroom a difficult learning environment. This argument is supported by Parsons who claims that girls and boys have different skills. Boys are good at problem solving while girls are good at communication. He suggests that the education system may be feminine as exams emphasise communication skills and lessons tend to be taught in a non-competitive way. Millard suggests that resources such as reading books benefit girls, and comics that boys prefer to read are banned from the classroom. This argument suggests that the education system benefits girls as it teaches both boys and girls in a feminine way and therefore causes boys to underachieve. **3** ☐

Feminist sociologists are extremely critical of the view that the education system causes male underachievement and claim that it actually causes female underachievement. They suggest that the education system is patriarchal and set up entirely for the benefit of men. Stanworth interviewed A Level students and found that teachers showed more interest and concern in their male students than in their female students. She also found that they were more likely to remember the names of male students. However, Stanworth's research was extremely subjective as she wanted to find evidence to support her theory. Spender conducted tape recordings of lessons and found that 60 per cent of lesson time was devoted to boys. She also found evidence of double standards in the judgements used to mark work for boys and girls. She found that boys received higher grades than girls for the same piece of work. Heaton and Lawson suggested that five things held girls back in education: a patriarchal curriculum, where boys dominated subjects such as ICT and hard sciences while girls were left in lessons such as textiles and languages; teachers' expectations that boys were more able than girls; boys' domination of space in ICT lessons and their abusive comments to girls; a lack of role models, with the majority being women in regular teaching jobs, and few as head teachers; and resources where girls were portrayed in subordinate roles to boys. **4** ☐

However, alternative sociological explanations suggest that females are not disadvantaged and it is factors outside the school which may be responsible for gender differences in educational achievement. The feminist movement has played a key part in raising the educational aspirations of females and this may have had a positive impact on their educational achievement. Research by Sue Sharpe provides evidence of this. She carried out a study on girls in 1976 and repeated the study in 1994. She found that in 1976 girls' priorities were marriage and motherhood but in 1994 this had changed and careers were then the priority. This change in female aspirations has been further encouraged through government equal opportunities policies. For example, GIST and WISE were introduced to further the aspirations and achievements of women in subjects such as science and engineering. **5** ☐ However, despite this change in female aspiration and achievement, women still earn less than men on average and have not yet achieved equality.

On the other hand, gender differences in educational achievement may not be due to girls doing better than they were previously but instead due to boys underperforming. **6** ☐ Evidence suggests that girls have always achieved more highly than boys. For example, in the 11+ exam the pass mark for girls was higher to ensure that a gender imbalance in grammar schools did not occur.

Mac an Ghaill suggests that underachievement among boys may be due to economic change. The transition to a service sector economy has meant a loss in traditional working-class male jobs and this may mean that due to unemployment, working-class males are suffering a crisis of masculinity. Working-class boys consequently lost interest in education as they could see their future was in unemployment or unskilled manual work like their fathers and brothers. They therefore searched for another source of status in anti-school subcultures where they received street credit for exclusion and rejecting teaching. However, Mac an Ghaill's research was conducted on a small sample in one geographical area and therefore the findings cannot be generalised to all working-class males. This also does not explain the fact that middle-class boys also underachieve in education compared with middle-class girls.

In considering sociological explanations for gender differences in education, it may be too simplistic to consider these in isolation without also looking at ethnicity and class. Girls do not outperform boys across the board; they only outperform boys from the same ethnic or class background. Statistics from the DfES (2004) show that middle-class boys outperform working-class girls and Indian boys outperform Bangladeshi girls. Warrington and Younger suggests that gender is the fifth most important factor which influences educational achievement, following prior attainment, class, ethnicity and quality of school. Therefore, although we can explore a range of sociological explanations for these differences, it is important not to place too much emphasis on the importance of gender in influencing educational achievement. **7** ☐

Examiner comments

a) A strong conclusion which introduces new evaluative material not previously mentioned. This would mean the candidate picks up marks for both knowledge and understanding (AO1) and evaluation (AO2b) in the last few lines of their answer.

b) A good understanding of the contribution of this theory to an understanding of gender differences and of the weaknesses of this theoretical approach. (AO1 and AO2b)

c) Good use of contemporary examples and linked to the educational policy aspect of the specification. (AO1)

d) An effective introduction which sets the scene for the question by referring to relevant and up-to-date statistical data. (AO1)

e) New paragraphs are well linked back to the question which will help the candidate capitalise on interpretation and application (AO2a) marks.

f) Effective use of key concepts, such as 'feminisation'. (AO1)

g) A good understanding of the contribution of feminist sociologists to understanding gender differences in education. (AO1 and AO2a)

Now try your own

Now try to write answers to the questions below. It is a good idea to try writing these answers under timed conditions. You should spend 45 minutes writing each answer.

- ◆ Outline and assess Marxist explanations of the relationship between education and work. (50 marks)
- ◆ Outline and assess the view that it is factors inside the school which affect the educational achievement of different ethnic groups. (50 marks)
- ◆ Outline and assess sociological explanations of the relationship between education and the economy. (50 marks)

Mass media

Revision checklist

You are at stage one of the revision process; the list below outlines all the topics and sub-topics which you need to cover in your revision. Take time now to make sure you have everything you need to revise this part of the course. The points referred to below can all be found in the core textbook. Your teacher(s) may also have taught you other sociological research studies, in which case you should also revise these. Tick off the areas once you have revised them and track your progress through the topics.

Defining and researching the mass media

Key concepts of the mass media including different forms of the media:

- Mass media (definition and examples) ☐
- Determinism (definition and explanation) ☐
- Censorship (definition, examples, arguments for and against censorship) ☐
- Research methods: content analysis (define, give examples, criticisms of the method) ☐
- Research methods: semiology (define, give examples, criticism of the method) ☐
- Research methods: experiments (define, give examples, criticism of the method) ☐

Ownership and control of the media: trends and patterns in media ownership and control

- Concentration (definition and examples) ☐
- Vertical integration (definition and examples) ☐
- Horizontal integration (definition and examples) ☐
- Transnational ownership (definition and examples) ☐
- Diversification (definition and examples) ☐
- Synergy (definition, examples and criticism) ☐

Theoretical explanations:

- Marxism (research studies, key concepts, evaluation) ☐
- Neo-Marxism (research studies, key concepts, evaluation) ☐
- Pluralism (research studies, key concepts, evaluation) ☐

Social construction of the news: process of news construction and the role of media owners, professionals and the state

- Owners (explanations and research studies of how they control news content) ☐
- Journalists (explanations, key concepts and research studies of how they control news content) ☐
- Editors (explanations, key concepts and research studies of how they control news content) ☐
- The state (explanations, evidence of constraints) ☐

Theoretical explanations:

- Marxism (analysis, research studies, key concepts and evaluation) ☐
- Neo-Marxism (analysis, research studies, key concepts and evaluation) ☐
- Pluralism (analysis, research studies, key concepts and evaluation) ☐
- Postmodern views (analysis, research studies, key concepts and evaluation) ☐

Media representation of social groups

- Gender (research studies, key concepts, explanations and evaluation) ☐
- Ethnicity (research studies, key concepts, explanations and evaluation) ☐
- Social class (research studies, key concepts, explanations and evaluation) ☐
- Age (research studies, key concepts, explanations and evaluation) ☐

Theoretical explanations:

- Marxism (analysis, research studies, key concepts and evaluation) ☐
- Neo-Marxism (analysis, research studies, key concepts and evaluation) ☐
- Pluralism (analysis, research studies, key concepts and evaluation) ☐
- Feminism (analysis, research studies, key concepts and evaluation) ☐
- Postmodern views (analysis, research studies, key concepts and evaluation) ☐

The effect of the media on society: influence of the media on the audience and the wider society

- Direct theories (definition, example of model types, research studies and evaluation) ☐
- Indirect theories (definition, example of model types, research studies and evaluation) ☐
- Marxism (research studies, key concepts and evaluation) ☐
- Neo-Marxism (research studies, key concepts and evaluation) ☐
- Interpretivism (research studies, key concepts and evaluation) ☐
- Postmodern views (research studies, key concepts and evaluation) ☐
- Deviancy amplification theories: moral panics (key concepts, research studies and analysis) ☐

Key concepts

This recap activity will ensure that you go over those all-important key concepts. Complete the key concept chart by writing a definition of the concept and, where possible, include which sociologist uses it. Refer to your core textbook or your classroom notes.

Key concepts	Definitions
Mass media	
Determinism	
Censorship	
Content analysis	
Semiology	
Experiments	
Traditional Marxists	
Neo-Marxist (hegemonic)	
Pluralism	
Agenda-setting	
Vertical integration	
Horizontal integration	
Transnational ownership	
GUMG	
Deviance amplification	
Direct theories (media effects)	
Indirect theories (media effects)	

Mix and match

revise

The purpose of this exercise is to test your knowledge of some of the key pieces of sociological research on the mass media. You will need to match the explanation of the research/theory with the name of the sociologist/title of the study. Identify the correct explanations by writing the correct letters in the blank boxes provided. Then check at the bottom of the page to see if you have matched them correctly.

Sociologist/title of study   Research/theory

Sociologist/title of study	Research/theory
I Uses and gratifications approach ☐	**A** The postmodern view put forth by this sociologist argues that the blurring between image and reality and global and local issues can lead to confusion about what is reality and what is hyper-reality. Individuals can pick and mix and create their own truth.
2 Biggs (1993) ☐	**B** This sociologist believes that representations of gender in the mass media have 'turned a corner'. Roles for males and females are becoming more equal; the television sitcom *Friends* is used to illustrate this point as both the male and female characters had equal coverage in terms of the storylines and both portrayed contemporary characteristics of gender.
3 Baudrillard (1988) ☐	**C** This classic study found the media to be guilty of unconscious racism: the negative language used towards ethnic minority groups and the way they were marginalised in the national press led to biased reporting by a dominant white press.
4 Hypodermic syringe model ☐	**D** This sociologist identifies three trends in the representation of ageing; increased number of older people appearing in soap operas, negative portrayals of old age in sitcoms, a move towards older people represented as being more active in leisure and society as a whole.
5 Van Dijk (1991) ☐	**E** Packard (1957) referred to the way the media has an immediate effect on its passive and uncritical audience. This theory believes that the audience is homogenous in the way it reads media messages.
6 Deviancy amplification theory ☐	**F** This term has been used by those who believe that exposure to violent content can have a positive effect on the individual; in watching or listening to violent content individuals can rid themselves of pent-up tension.
7 Gauntlett (2008) ☐	**G** This approach argues that the audience uses the media and is active in how it reads media messages. It is the audience who selects media for their own purpose and to satisfy their own individual need.
8 Catharsis ☐	**H** This term is used to explain how the media can be instrumental in strengthening and magnifying deviance within society. The media firstly heightens public awareness and concern and then escalates the problem by increasing participation in it by the attention the media has given to the initial situation or concern.

Answers: 1. G, 2. D, 3. A, 4. E, 5. C, 6. H, 7. B, 8. F

Check your knowledge quick fire quiz

This multiple choice quiz will test your knowledge of the mass media. Each question will be worth a number of points; the points are indicated at the end of the question. The more points a question is worth, the more difficult it is: the top mark questions reflect whether you have read your core textbook thoroughly. Once you have ticked the answer you believe to be correct, add up your score to reveal whether you are a mass media expert!

I *Who argued that the mass media is the main 'leisure time interest' in society, providing people with more of a 'shared environment' than any other institution?* **(3 points)**

- a) ☐ McQuail (2000)
- b) ☐ McNeil (2000)
- c) ☐ Denscombe (2000)

2 *McLuhan (1964) uses this concept to describe how the media, as a force of social change, can fundamentally affect how people experience their lives.* **(4 points)**

- a) ☐ 'Media manipulation'
- b) ☐ 'Media determinism'
- c) ☐ 'Media fundamentalism'

3 *Which research method is commonly used in the study of 'media effects' on the audience?* **(3 points)**

- a) ☐ Case study
- b) ☐ Semiotic analysis
- c) ☐ Experiments

4 *What term can be used to explain how the media has come to be owned by fewer organisations, which has resulted in larger companies buying up smaller companies, or merging to increase their percentage of media ownership?* **(3 points)**

- a) ☐ Diversification
- b) ☐ Concentration
- c) ☐ Vertical integration

5 *Trends in recent ownership have become a particular concern of many campaigns promoting the need for a more accountable British media. Which of the following is campaigning for a more diverse, democratic British media?* **(4 points)**

- a) ☐ Campaign for Press & Broadcasting Freedom (CPBF)
- b) ☐ Campaign for Press & Fair and Balanced Freedom (CPFBF)
- c) ☐ Campaign for Press & Broadcasting (CPB)

6 *Whose study titled the 'Policing the crisis' found that the media supported the police and the legal structures at a time when the general public were beginning to ask questions about the role the police played in society?* **(3 points)**

- a) ☐ Van Dijk (1991)
- b) ☐ P. Gilroy (1995)
- c) ☐ S. Hall et al. (1995)

7 *Which theoretical perspective argues that the media are a positive force which can be described as the 'fourth estate', whose role it is to protect democracy and to keep a watchful eye over the other 'three estates': government, parliament and the judiciary?* **(4 points)**

- a) ☐ Positivism
- b) ☐ Pluralism
- c) ☐ New right

(continued)

8 *Galtung and Ruge's idea of 'news values' has been criticised by many sociologists. Stuart Hall criticises Galtung and Ruge (1970) from a neo-Marxist perspective; what is his main concern?* **(3 points)**

a) ☐ Journalists are the ones who construct the news; they construct statements in which the news makes sense

b) ☐ News values fails to shed light on the ideological factors influencing them

c) ☐ Galtung and Ruge's idea of news values is outdated and does not apply to contemporary journalism

9 *Who argued that the 'news diary' was an important factor in creating the content of the news?* **(2 points)**

a) ☐ S. Hall (1995)

b) ☐ Bagdikian (2000)

c) ☐ Schlesinger (1987)

10 *Which theoretical perspective believes that owners benefit from capitalism and therefore ensure that their media forms support and promote capitalism, thus arguing that media owners directly manipulate the content of the media?* **(3 points)**

a) ☐ Neo-Marxist (hegemonic)

b) ☐ Postmodernist

c) ☐ Traditional Marxist

Possible 32 points

26–32 Well done! You are a mass media genius!

19–25 It's official: you are definitely becoming a sociology star!

11–18 Looks like you might be avoiding the more difficult questions – get back to reading that textbook!

0–10 Oh dear, you're not going to win any 'sociology student of the year' prizes!

Answers: 1.a, 2.b, 3.c, 4.b, 5.a, 6.c, 7.b, 8.b, 9.c, 10.c

Theory identifier

The statements below reflect the viewpoints of one of the following theories: traditional Marxism, neo-Marxism, pluralism or postmodernism. Identify which theory goes with which statement by writing in the space above the statement.

1 _____

This theory includes members from the Centre for Contemporary Cultural Studies (CCCS). The CCCS have analysed the way in which media professionals create media products that reflect and reinforce the power structures of society. They believe that this happens without direct influence from media owners.

2 _____

This theory believes that owners directly manipulate media content, it is in the owner's interest to maintain the status quo, and they are a distinct group with a privileged lifestyle which benefits from the capitalist system.

3 _____

This theory believes that we are living in an era of the 'end of meaning'. News has become more entertainment-based and focuses on the narrative of news stories rather than factual evidence; the term 'infotainment' has been used to describe this process.

4 _____

This theory is supported by media professionals; however, there is little empirical evidence to support the theory. The theory simply argues that there is choice and diversity of media products and that any bias in media production is a response to the demands of the audience.

5 _____

This theory sees the state as exercising considerable control over the content of the news though informal and formal social control.

6 _____

This theory believes that media professionals exercise objectivity and a sense of responsibility in their news production. Media professionals are aware of their audiences' interests and will respond to these when constructing the news.

7 _____

This theory is concerned with the ways in which the media function to control society through ideology, they are particularly concerned with how the media represents social class and believe that the media is instrumental in perpetuating 'false class consciousnesses'.

8 _____

This theory believes that the media has been instrumental in promoting a 'pick and mix' culture. By representing a variety of images, people are able to choose from a number of representations to form their own identity and lifestyle.

9 _____

This theory uses the term 'hegemony' to explain how the ruling class norms and values are maintained. This theory recognises that social inequality goes beyond the issues of social class and that the media enforce hegemonic ideology by representing social groups in a narrow and marginalised way.

Answers: 1. neo-Marxism, 2. traditional Marxism, 3. postmodernism, 4. pluralism, 5. neo-Marxism, 6. pluralism, 7. traditional Marxism, 8. postmodernism, 9. neo-Marxism

Applying research studies task

revise

The following is a list of some of the key concepts you may need to refer to when answering questions on the mass media unit. Fill in the spaces in the adjacent column with details of a sociologist/theorist and their research/theory which could be used to illustrate each concept. The first one is done for you. Answers can be found at the back of the book.

Key concepts	Sociologist/research/theory
Ideological state apparatus (ISA)	Neo-Marxist Althusser used this term to describe institutions whose purpose it was to maintain hegemony by shaping society's norms and values.
Repressive state apparatus (RSA)	
Moral panic	
Hyper-reality	
News values	
'Hierarchy of credibility'	
News diary	
Global village	
'Malestream'	
Hypodermic syringe model	
Catharsis	
Two-step flow model	
Uses and gratification model	
'Folk devils'	
Hegemony	

ExamCafé

Power and control: mass media

The skills you have gained at AS level must also be applied to your A2 exam responses. It is very important that you not only refresh your memory of the necessary skills but that you are also aware of how many marks you could potentially be awarded for each skill. These marks are summarised below:

◆ AO1 Knowledge and understanding = 23 marks
◆ AO2a Interpretation and application = 10 marks
◆ AO2b Analysis and evaluation = 17 marks

Total marks = 50

Exam answer-based activity

The answer below is an example of a well-written response to a G673 mass media question. Your task is to match the examiner's comments listed at the bottom with the numbers listed in the body of the exam answer. You must correctly match the lettered examiner comments with the numbered points. You can then check at the bottom of the page to see if you have matched them correctly. The purpose of this activity is to give you an awareness of the key points which are required to answer this question and of where the skills of AO1, AO2a and AO2b are being used.

Outline and assess the traditional Marxist view that media owners directly manipulate media content. (50 marks)

rewind

Student answer

There are a number of theories relating to the influence of media owners on the content of their media forms, including both Marxist and pluralist views. There has been an increase in concern about the influence of media owners; this is due to the trend towards media ownership being concentrated into fewer hands. Bagdikian (2000) argued that if the USA's media were owned by separate people there would be 25,000 owners. Instead, only 10 huge corporations own everything. The traditional Marxist view is particularly concerned about statistics of ownership such as Bagdikian's; for traditional Marxists, the owners of such huge corporations should be monitored and regulated more closely. The aim of this essay is to outline and address the concerns of the traditional Marxists and critique the view by considering the alternative neo-Marxist view and the pluralist view of media ownership. **1** ☐

The manipulative model of media ownership draws on traditional Marxists' theory: they believe that the capitalist class and the government are only concerned with representing their own interests and that they act in a conscious and direct way. As the media owners of huge corporations are a part of the capitalist class, they directly control the mass media to benefit themselves (Moore et al., 2006). Rupert Murdoch, a media mogul who is a transnational owner, has been accused of trying to directly manipulate his own media content. It was alleged that Murdoch directly threatened the former Prime Minister, Tony Blair, on the issue of Europe. It was claimed that Murdoch told Tony Blair that if he did not encourage the government to have a more critical view on Europe, then the *Sun* newspaper would switch its allegiance from Labour to the Conservative party. Such alleged behaviour at the time earned Murdoch the title of the 'Phantom Prime Minister'. Furthermore, in 2003 the *Guardian* newspaper noted that Murdoch at the time owned 175 newspapers which mirrored the Republican views of Rupert Murdoch. Murdoch himself supported the military action against Saddam Hussein and this was the view that was portrayed in all the 175 newspapers. **2** ☐

The influence of Murdoch is even more troubling for traditional Marxists due to another media ownership trend of horizontal integration. Rupert Murdoch's company, News Corporation, owns media forms such as newspapers and television networks which include FOX news in the USA. Walter Cronkite's hard-hitting 2004 documentary 'Outfoxed: Rupert Murdoch's war on journalism' attempts to expose the FOX news network as being a Republican propaganda machine. Cronkite's evidence of Fox memos sent direct from Rupert Murdoch instructing news editors, reporters and anchors on what to cover in the news can be used to support the traditional Marxist view. **3** ☐

However, the conspiratorial view put forth by the traditional Marxists has been contested by such writers as Negrine (1989), who argues that much of the evidence cited to support owners as direct manipulators is largely anecdotal and therefore cannot be generalised to all media owners. However, there is an alternative Marxist viewpoint put forth by the neo-Marxists. The neo-Marxists are concerned with the role culture plays in perpetuating inequalities, and are particularly concerned with how the ruling capitalist class culture is portrayed as the dominant and superior form of culture. The term 'hegemony' is used by the neo-Marxists to try and explain how the media plays a key role in reinforcing a particular set of ideas; these ideas are made up from the capitalist class culture. Neo-Marxists look beyond the influence of the media owners and believe that it lies with the media professionals, who are mainly from upper-middle-class families and have attended institutions such as public schools, which actively reinforce capitalist hegemony. Unlike traditional Marxists, the neo-Marxists (also known as the hegemonic model) do not believe that the manipulation of the media by media professionals is a conscious act; they believe that it is an unconscious act which stems from the attitudes of the people who work in the media, that the background of the media professionals influences their views. Views and opinions that stand outside the limited and narrow view of these media professionals will be presented as inferior. **4** ☐

The Glasgow University Media Group (GUMG) found evidence to support the neo-Marxist hegemonic model. GUMG found that media professionals constantly projected their own common assumptions while marginalising the views of others. In one famous GUMG study of the industrial dispute between the miners and their managers in the 1980s, it was found that the managers were always interviewed in controlled and calm environments, while the strikers were interviewed on the picket lines surrounded by noise and chaos; thus the former were seen as being reasonable and the latter as unreasonable and deviant. There have been many criticisms of the neo-Marxist view as it fails to recognise the increase in female and ethnic representation evident in the new media professionals. Furthermore, with the developments in media technology, individuals are able to produce professional-quality media products which can be broadcast on video-sharing websites such as YouTube. **5** ☐

The traditional Marxist view and the neo-Marxist view have been criticised by pluralists. Pluralists do not believe that the media owners or professionals directly or indirectly influence the media, instead it is the audience which dictates media content. They believe that the nature of 'bias' is determined by the audience; the media that is available is a result of what the people want. This idea can be applied to the increase of reality-style television programmes such as *Big Brother*, *The Family* and *The X Factor*; such shows get high viewing figures, supporting the view that it is the audience that determines media content, not the media owners or media professionals. Furthermore, in contrast to the traditional Marxist view, pluralists argue that trends in media ownership such as concentration can bring benefits for the consumer. Collins and Murroni (1996) argue that large-sized media organisations tend to bring the resources required for comprehensive high-quality viewing. **6** ☐

In conclusion there are many different theoretical views on the influence of media owners and professionals on media content. The traditional Marxist manipulative model focuses on the direct influence of media owners, whereas the neo-Marxist model focuses on how hegemonic culture is transmitted by middle-class media professionals. Alternatively, the pluralists' view states that it is in fact the audience which is active and therefore it is the audience which determines media. However, the pluralist view fails to recognise that diversity and choice can be limited by the advertisers: the growth in reality TV could simply be a product of clever media marketing rather than a response to audience interest. The traditional Marxist view raises many relevant concerns; however, it fails to fully explain how it would be possible for someone like Rupert Murdoch, who is a global media owner, to directly and consciously manipulate all of his various media forms throughout the globe. **7** ☐

Examiner comments

a) The response includes a brief summary of the main theoretical views which relate to answering the question. The question is referred back to and contemporary examples are used to support the summary and final evaluation of each theoretical perspective. On the whole this is a sound conclusion to an essay answer which is rich in the three main skills of AO1, AO2a and AO2b.

b) This part of the response has outlined and explained the main theory linked to the questions. There is some use of relevant evidence to support the theoretical view, although this could have been developed further. The response would gain marks for AO1 and AO2a.

c) Another link into an alternative theoretical perspective, showing a wide-ranging knowledge of the theories linked to media ownership. Some illustration of the pluralist perspective, although the point relating to the audience being active in the content of the media could have been illustrated further. Points here would be gained for AO1 and AO2a.

d) Good use of evidence which includes further research in the form of documentaries. This part of the response has also included other relevant concepts linked to trends in media ownership. This part would gain marks for AO2a.

e) The response clearly introduces the concerns of the theoretical view outline in the question. It also shows some awareness of opposing views. Furthermore, the response contextualises the issue by referring to relevant statistics. The paragraph successfully sets the scene for the rest of the essay. The response would gain marks for AO1.

f) Good use of relevant evidence which has been contextualised. Relevant use of contemporary examples such as YouTube. Some evidence of evaluation. This part of the response would get marks for AO2a and AO2b

g) Good outline of alternative Marxist view showing clear understanding of the difference between the two Marxist perspectives. However, examples could have been used to illustrate the alternative theory. This part of the response would gain marks for AO1 and AO2b.

Answers: 1.e, 2.b, 3.d, 4.g, 5.f, 6.c, 7.a

Now try your own

Now try to write answers to the questions below. It is a good idea to try writing these answers under timed conditions. You should spend 45 minutes writing each answer.

- ◆ Outline and assess the view that state regulation of the media should be reduced. (50 marks)
- ◆ Outline and assess feminist views of how the media reinforces gender stereotypes. (50 marks)
- ◆ Outline and assess the view that the media has a direct and conscious effect on the audience. (50 marks)

Power and politics

Revision checklist

You are at stage one of the revision process; the list below outlines all the topics and sub-topics which you need to cover in your revision. Take time now to make sure you have everything you need to revise this part of the course. The points referred to below can all be found in the core textbook. Your teacher(s) may also have taught you other sociological research studies in which case you should also revise these. Tick off the areas once you have revised them and track your progress through the topics.

Defining and exploring political action in society

Different types of political action:
- Political parties (definition and examples) ☐
- Pressure groups (definition and examples) ☐
- New social movements (definition and examples) ☐
- Direct and indirect action (definition and explanation) ☐
- Terrorism (definition and examples) ☐
- Riots (definition and examples) ☐
- Demonstrations and strikes (definition and examples) ☐
- Lobbying (definition and examples) ☐
- Cybernetworking (definition, explanation and analysis) ☐

Participation in, and emergence of, new social movements

- Social movements (definition, analysis and evaluation) ☐
- Membership of new social movements (examples and analysis) ☐

Theoretical perspectives:
- Collective behaviour/identity (key concepts, research studies and evaluation) ☐
- Marxism (key concepts, research studies and evaluation) ☐
- Postmodern views (key concepts, research studies and evaluation) ☐
- Globalisation (key concepts, research studies, examples and evaluation) ☐

The changing patterns of political action

- Types of political action including: ballot box, new social movements (key concepts, research studies and evaluation) ☐
- Globalisation (key concepts, research studies and evaluation) ☐

Theoretical views of political action:
- Marxism (key concepts, research studies and analysis) ☐
- Feminism (key concepts, research studies and analysis) ☐
- Pluralism (key concepts and research studies) ☐
- Postmodern views (key concepts and research studies) ☐
- Collective behaviour/identity (key concepts, research studies and analysis) ☐

Political ideologies and their relationship to political action

- Ideologies (definition) ☐
- Political ideology (definition, key concepts and research studies) ☐
- Liberalism (definition, key concepts, research studies, examples linked to political action, evaluation) ☐
- Conservatism (definition, key concepts, research studies, examples linked to political action, evaluation) ☐
- Neo-conservatism (definition, key concepts, research studies, examples linked to political action and evaluation. Fundamentalism should also be covered under this ideology. ☐

- Feminism (definition, key concepts, research studies, examples linked to political action, evaluation) ☐
- Anarchism (definition, key concepts, research studies, examples linked to political action, evaluation) ☐

The nature and distribution of political power in society

- Power (definition and evaluation of definition)
- ☐

Distribution of power in relation to the following:

- The state (definition, examples) ☐
- Government (definition, research studies, analysis) ☐
- The media (definition, research studies, analysis) ☐
- Transnational corporations (TNCs) (definition, examples, research studies, analysis) ☐
- Businesses (examples, research studies, analysis) ☐
- Individuals (examples, research studies, analysis) ☐

Theoretical views on how political power is distributed:

- Weberian (key concepts, explanation, evaluation) ☐
- Functionalist (key concepts, explanation, evaluation) ☐
- Neo-liberalist (key concepts, explanation, evaluation) ☐
- Pluralism (key concepts, explanation, evaluation) ☐
- Elite theory (definition, key concepts, research studies, evaluation) ☐
- Marxist theory (key concepts, explanation, evaluation) ☐
- Neo-Marxist theory (key concepts, explanation, evaluation) ☐
- Postmodern views (key concepts, explanation, research studies, and evaluation) ☐

Key concepts

This recap activity will ensure that you go over those all-important key concepts. Complete the key concept chart by writing a definition of the concept and, where possible, include which sociologist uses it. Refer to your core textbook or your classroom notes.

Key concepts	Definitions
Political parties	
Pressure groups	
New social movements	
Terrorism	
Lobbying	
Cybernetworking	
Transnational corporations (TNCs)	
Democracy	
Oligarchy	
Direct action	
Anarchism	

Mix and match

revise

The purpose of this exercise is to test your knowledge of some of the key pieces of sociological research on power and politics. You will need to match the explanation of the research/theory with the name of the sociologist/title of the study. Identify the correct explanations by writing the correct letters in the blank boxes provided. Then check at the bottom of the page to see if you have matched them correctly.

Sociologist/title of study   Research/theory

1 Elite theory ☐

2 Jowett (2001) ☐

3 Anarchism ☐

4 Lukes (1974) ☐

5 Keddie (1999) ☐

6 Conservatism ☐

7 Mackintosh and Mooney (2000) ☐

8 Individualism ☐

A
This belief is central to the liberal ideology. Societies should recognise the uniqueness of the individual.

B
This theory parallels that of functionalist sociology. The family is of importance for the theorists as they believe that the family teaches individuals shared beliefs and values.

C
This sociologist believes that fundamentalism can be regarded as a new religious politics and can be a focus for resistance to racism.

D
These two neo-Marxists emphasis three crucial themes to Marxist ideology.

E
This feminist wrote the article titled 'Is feminism still important?' This looked at the relevance of feminism 30 years after the second wave.

F
This theory believes that societies could and should exist without the evil and coercive power of the state.

G
This sociologist argues that power has 'three faces'. The first accepts that political power is evident in the outcomes achieved; the second sees power in terms of what is removed from decision making; and the third sees power in terms of the ability of some to shape the thoughts and desires of others.

H
This theory believes that people with power possess superior personal qualities that make them best suited to rule.

Check your knowledge quick fire quiz

This multiple choice quiz will test your knowledge of the topic of power and politics. Each question will be worth a number of points; the points are indicated at the end of the question. The more points a question is worth, the more difficult it is: the top mark questions reflect whether you have read your core textbook thoroughly. Once you have ticked the answer you believe to be correct, add up your score to reveal whether you are a power and politics expert!

1 *Which theorist wrote that authority was of three different types; traditional, charismatic or legal?* **(3 points)**

a) ☐ Marx

b) ☐ Weber

c) ☐ Parsons

2 *The pressure group the 'Confederation of British Industry' was formed in what year?* **(4 points)**

a) ☐ 1963

b) ☐ 1965

c) ☐ 1969

3 *Which country was the first to undergo an industrial revolution after the increase in the use of machines in the textile industry led to workers losing their jobs?* **(3 points)**

a) ☐ England

b) ☐ America

c) ☐ France

4 *What are the two classifications of new social movements by Habermas?* **(3 points)**

a) ☐ Norm-oriented/value-oriented

b) ☐ Single issue/multi-issue

c) ☐ Defensive/offensive

5 *What is one of the main criticisms of the collective behaviour explanation of social movements?* **(4 points)**

a) ☐ That it is too vague in its view of society

b) ☐ It's a static view; it assumes that the existing political institutions are able to meet the demands of the people

c) ☐ The theory is too close to Marxism and sees political upheaval as a result of capitalism

6 *Which social commentator argues that new social movements offer an alternative political order based on forms of mass participation in which people have a greater engagement with the issues they are supporting?* **(3 points)**

a) ☐ Hallsworth (1994)

b) ☐ Giddens (2006)

c) ☐ Nash (2000)

7 *Which feminist argues that the umbrella term 'women' should be abandoned?* **(4 points)**

a) ☐ Butler (1990)

b) ☐ Hirst (1993)

c) ☐ Gilligan (1982)

(continued)

8 *Which theory sees no place for new social movements as they believe that there exists a range of political parties and pressure groups in society which cater for all beliefs?* **(4 points)**

a) ☐ Neo-Marxism

b) ☐ Feminism

c) ☐ Pluralism

9 *Who stated that political ideology is a set of logical political ideas that provide a plan of action?* **(3 points)**

a) ☐ Saunders (1983)

b) ☐ Heywood (2001)

c) ☐ Westergaard and Resler (1976)

10 *What does Bell warn us against in his book?* **(4 points)**

a) ☐ New social movements

b) ☐ Globalisation and its effects

c) ☐ Ideology and its effects

Possible 35 points

26–35 Well done! You are a power and politics expert!

19–25 It's official: you are becoming a sociology star!

11–18 Looks like you might be avoiding the more difficult questions – get back to reading that textbook!

0–10 Oh dear, you're not going to win any 'sociology student of the year' prizes!

Answers: 1.b, 2.b, 3.a, 4.c, 5.b, 6.a, 7.a, 8.c, 9.b, 10.c

Theory identifier

The statements below reflect the viewpoints of one of the following theories:
Marxism, neo-Marxism, postmodernism, collective behaviour/identity or globalisation.
Identify which theory goes with which statement by writing in the space above
the statement.

1 _____

This theory was a product of the USA and viewed social movements as dangerous and dysfunctional resulting in a strain on society. This theory owes a lot of its thinking to the functionalist perspective; like functionalism it believed that in a healthy society there was no need for social movements as political participation through traditional political channels adequately played a function in representing society's political views.

2 _____

Commentators of this theory, such as Klein (2000), believe that diversity and choice are being crushed by big business and that people have lost the opportunity to 'pick and mix' their identity as big businesses invest in certain brands and through global marketing persuade consumers to buy only certain brands and images.

3 _____

The traditional view of this theory was unable to explain the rise of new social movements. However, supporters of this theory, such as Offe (1985), believe that the fundamentals of the theory can be used to explain how NSMs are a response to the growing dominance of capitalism: they have formed to try and reverse the deprivations caused by capitalist societies.

4 _____

This theory attempts to explain how multinational and transnational corporations (MNCs and TNCs) now dominate culture. People have become increasingly concerned about the growth of global corporations and have begun to make a stand; they have joined transnational social movements to try and oppose both MNCs and TNCs.

5 _____

Supporters of this theory, such as Castells (1983), tried to explain the political actions of social movements. For Castells, urban social movements united people who wished to either defend or challenge their local environment or public service provision.

6 _____

One of the key writers of this theory, Gramsci (1971), argued that for the ruling classes to maintain their hold on society they must secure the consent of the masses by instilling in them its own ideas; this process is known as hegemony.

7 _____

This theory uses the concept of discourse to try and explain how power is enforced. This theory believes that a discourse is a taken-for-granted way of doing and thinking about something. There are within our society 'expert discourses' which have a superior status; power within society operates within such discourses which restricts alternatives and so becomes a form of social control.

8 _____

This theory believes that social movements are not necessarily a response to coping with risk but instead a way for members to develop a self-image. Supporters of this theory, such as Melucci (1989), argue that supporters of new social movements are more concerned about the lifestyle of being part of the movement than the issues they are campaigning for. Membership of the movement acts as a sign to others and is a mark of identity.

Answers: 1. collective behaviour theory, 2. postmodernism, 3. Marxism, 4. globalisation, 5. Marxism, 6. neo-Marxism, 7. postmodernism, 8. collective identity theory

Applying research studies task

The following is a list of some of the key concepts you may need to refer to when answering questions on the power and politics unit. Fill in the spaces in the adjacent column with details of a sociologist/theorist and their research/theory, or a description of the concept, which could be used to illustrate each concept. The first one is done for you. Answers can be found at the back of the book.

Key concepts	Sociologist/research/theory
Cyberocracy	Ronfeldt (1992) believed that new technologies such as the Internet gave grassroots activists the opportunity to challenge undemocratic political regimes.
Resource mobilisation theory (RMT)	
Risk society	
Global imperialism	
McJobs	
Culture jamming	
Eco-warriors	
Cyber-balkanisation	
Social movement organisations (SMOs)	
Meritocracies	

ExamCafé

Power and control: power and politics

The skills you have gained at AS level must also be applied to your A2 exam responses. It is very important that you not only refresh your memory of the necessary skills but that you are also aware of how many marks you could potentially be awarded for each skill. These marks are summarised below:

◆ AO1 Knowledge and understanding = 23 marks
◆ AO2a Interpretation and application = 10 marks
◆ AO2b Analysis and evaluation = 17 marks
Total marks = 50

Exam answer-based activity

The answer below is an example of a well-written response to a G673 power and politics question. Your task is to match the examiner's comments listed at the bottom with the numbers listed in the body of the exam answer. You must correctly match the lettered examiner comments with the numbered points. You can then check at the bottom of the page to see if you have matched them correctly. The purpose of this activity is to give you an awareness of the key points which are required to answer this question and of where the skills of AO1, AO2a and AO2b are being used.

Outline and assess the view by collective identity theorists that new social movements' engagement in political action is superficial. (50 marks)

rewind

Student answer

The collective identity theory is one of several theories which try to explain the changing patterns of political action. Collective identity theory has evolved out of the new era of post-modernity. New social movements (NSMs) are informal without any distinct hierarchal structure. NSMs vary in size and can be distinguished by the fact that they often act outside established political groups; one example of this is the Greenpeace movement which was founded in 1971. It was originally set up in protest against the US nuclear weapons testing which was taking place in Alaska. The collective identity theory has a very pessimistic outlook on the purpose of NSMs, believing that they are merely superficial and that the members of NSMs are more concerned with the positive self-image that is projected through membership than the actual cause of the NSM. This essay will assess this view by referring to arguments which support the view that NSMs have been instrumental in direct and successful action; some consideration will also be paid to alternative theoretical views of NSMs. **1** ☐

Melucci (1989) supports the view put forth by the collective identity theory by stating that for the supporters of NSMs, the issue they are campaigning for is not as important as the lifestyle that goes with being a member of a NSM: he believes that membership signifies a mark of identity. Melucci sees NSMs as merely 'social movement networks' and says that their engagement in political action is shallow and without substance. Melucci goes on to say that even though individual members of NSMs through membership develop a collective identity, this collective identity is not fixed with a high self-esteem image. Melucci concludes by stating that he believes that NSMs are informal networks of individuals linked by cultural contact but not by fixed shared interests or ideologies. However, Melucci's theory can be challenged by the Reclaim the Streets (RTS) social movement which was founded in London in 1991. Its members had a shared interest, mainly in the prevention of traffic congestion. The movement started as small localised groups at first, which were interested in promoting a healthy lifestyle through encouraging people to walk and cycle and if necessary to use free public transport and to oppose the use of cars. Their action was far from superficial as their direct action methods included DIY cycle lanes painted at night, 'subvertising' billboard car advertisements and disrupting the Earls Court Motor Show. **2** ☐

Sociologists such as Wilson (1971) argue that social movements are distinct but can be defined in various ways. Wilson believes them to be organised attempts to either block or promote social change using conscious and collective action. However, there has been a distinction made between traditional and new social movements: new social movements have evolved out of changes within Western societies, including social and economic changes, such as changes in the economy, e.g. the shift from the secondary sector to the service sector. In this way it could be argued that NSMs are not superficial but are an active challenge against representative democracy, which has increased due to the fact that people have continued to lose confidence and trust in traditional party politics. However, Melucci's idea that NSMs are fluid and not fixed in terms of membership can be supported further by Gorringe and Rosier's (2008) study of demonstrators at the 'Make Poverty History' (MPH) march in July 2005. Those that joined the protest came from diverse backgrounds, including members of institutions such as the teachers' union and members of Christian and Muslim religions. What they had in common was their interest in the cause; their lifestyles and beliefs were not uniformed and fixed. **3** ☐

The pluralist perspective takes the criticisms of NSMs further by arguing that there is no need for NSMs, as there is adequate representation of different views in the political parties and pressure groups that already exist within society. Hirst supports this view by arguing that because NSMs are so fragmented and members are so loosely connected, they make little difference and are powerless. Any changes that they do make will be limited; they do not have the clout to bring about radical change. In short, the pluralists believe NSMs to be not only superficial but of no real value to society as a whole. **4** ☐

In conclusion, from considering the evidence, NSMs have been involved in direct action even if it is simply at the level of social awareness; they have been instrumental in bringing many issues to public and political attention. People coming together from diverse backgrounds in the name of a single cause, such as the MPH protests, cannot be written off as superficial. Melucci's pessimistic view of membership of NSMs simply being used as a mark of self-image and identity undermines the work done by NSMs. **5** ☐

Examiner comments

a) Relevant use of evidence and application of the theory. Good use of evaluation, relevant examples used to explain the direct action of NSMs and necessary key concepts also referred to. Marks gained for AO1, AO2a and AO2b.

b) This is a good start: the student has defined key terms and has set out the intentions of the essay. Furthermore, there is some evidence of knowledge and understanding and application of a relevant NSM. Marks gained in AO1 and AO2a.

c) Response attempts to evaluate the argument posed in the question, some use of relevant evidence, linking in sociological research. Good use of another example of an NSM, which has been applied in the context of the question set. Marks gained for AO2a and AO2b.

d) Response develops the argument further by evaluating the question set by the use of an alternative theoretical perspective. This adds another dimension to the argument, although examples could have been used to illustrate the pluralist view. Marks gained for AO1 and AO2b.

e) A brief summary which attempts to address the question. Although the other views brought out in the body of the argument could have been recapped, marks would be gained for AO2b.

Now try your own

Now try to write answers to the questions below. It is a good idea to try writing these answers under timed conditions. You should spend 45 minutes writing each answer.

◆ Outline and assess Marxist explanations of the distribution of political power within capitalist societies. (50 marks)

◆ Outline and assess the success of new social movements in changing political thought. (50 marks)

◆ Outline and assess the view that traditional political parties have lost the support and trust of the people. (50 marks)

Answers: 1.b, 2.a, 3.c, 4.d, 5.e

Exploring social inequality and difference

Revision checklist

You are at stage one of the revision process; the list below outlines all the topics and sub-topics which you need to cover in your revision. Take time now to make sure you have everything you need to revise this part of the course. The points referred to below can all be found in the core textbook. Your teacher(s) may also have taught you other sociological research studies in which case you should also revise these. Tick off the areas once you have revised them and track your progress through the topics.

Patterns and trends of inequality and difference related to:

- Social class (concepts, statistics and sociological research evidence to explain social class inequalities in relation to 4 topic areas including the workplace) ☐
- Gender (concepts, statistics and sociological research evidence to explain gender inequalities in relation to 4 topic areas including the workplace) ☐
- Ethnicity (concepts, statistics and sociological research evidence to explain ethnic inequalities in relation to 4 topic areas including the workplace) ☐
- Age (concepts, statistics and sociological research evidence to explain age inequalities in relation to 4 topic areas including the workplace) ☐

Theoretical explanations of the patterns and trends in relation to social class and evaluation of these

- Functionalism ☐
- Marxism ☐
- Neo-Marxism ☐
- Weberianism ☐
- Feminism ☐
- Postmodernism ☐

Sociological explanations of the changing class structure

- Upper class (theories, research studies, concepts and evaluation) ☐
- Middle class (theories, research studies, concepts and evaluation) ☐
- Working class (theories, research studies, concepts and evaluation) ☐
- Underclass (theories, research studies, concepts and evaluation) ☐

Theoretical explanations of the patterns and trends in relation to gender and evaluation of these

- Functionalism ☐
- Marxism ☐
- Weberianism ☐
- Liberal feminism ☐
- Marxist feminism ☐
- Radical feminism ☐
- Black feminism ☐
- Third wave feminism ☐

Theoretical explanations of the patterns and trends in relation to ethnicity and evaluation of these

- Functionalism ☐
- Marxism ☐
- Neo-Marxism ☐
- Weberianism ☐
- Postmodernism ☐

Theoretical explanations of the patterns and trends in relation to age and evaluation of these

- Functionalism ☐
- Marxism ☐
- Weberianism ☐
- Postmodernism ☐

The interrelationship between class, gender, ethnicity and age ☐

ExamCafé

Question guidance
Exploring social inequality and difference

The skills you have gained at AS level must also be applied to your A2 exam responses. It is very important that you not only refresh your memory of the necessary skills, but that you are also aware of how many marks you could potentially be awarded for each skill.

Question 1

Question 1 will be related to the study of sociological research.
For question 1 you could be awarded the following marks:

- AO1 Knowledge and understanding = 10 marks
- AO2a Interpretation and application = 5 marks

Total marks = 15

In this question you will be asked to use the item and your own knowledge in your answer. You are expected to make at least three main points. The question will draw on your knowledge of sociological research. You do not need to evaluate in this answer.

You should spend approximately 15 minutes answering this part of the question.

Question 2

Question 2 will be related to the study of sociological research.
For question 2 you could be awarded the following marks:

- AO1 Knowledge and understanding = 5 marks
- AO2a Interpretation and application = 5 marks
- AO2b Analysis and evaluation = 15 marks

Total marks = 25

In this question you should write in an evaluative way presenting evidence which would both agree and disagree with the statement in the question. The question will draw on your understanding of sociological research and the appropriateness of different methodological approaches. It will be related to the summary of a piece of research provided in the source material on the exam paper. You should particularly consider the aim of the research and the context of the study. Your answer should contain references to a range of methodological concepts. (These are outlined in this book.) Your response should be in the form of an essay with a clear introduction and conclusion.

You should spend approximately 30 minutes answering this part of the question.

Question 3/4a

Question 3 or 4 part (a) will be related to the study of social class, gender, ethnicity or age inequalities.
For question 3 or 4 part (a) you could be awarded the following marks:

◆ AO1 Knowledge and understanding = 15 marks
◆ AO2a Interpretation and application = 5 marks

Total marks = 20

In this question you should present evidence to support the question in the form of research studies, statistics, concepts and theories. When referring to statistics you should also quote the date and source of these. You do not need to make evaluative comments in this part of the question.

This question will assess your ability to think sociologically and holistically and should draw on material from a range of sociological areas/topics covered. (You should refer to at least four different topic areas.)

You should spend approximately 20 minutes answering this part of the question.

Question 3/4b

Question 3 or 4 part (b) will be related to the study of social class, gender, ethnicity or age inequalities.
For question 3 or 4 part (b) you could be awarded the following marks:

◆ AO1 Knowledge and understanding = 15 marks
◆ AO2a Interpretation and application = 5 marks
◆ AO2b Analysis and evaluation = 20 marks

Total marks = 40

In this question you should write in an evaluative way assessing the theories on the topic in the question. You should aim to write about all relevant theories and include references to sociological research and concepts. In order to maximise the marks you are awarded for AO2b analysis and evaluation, you should also aim to evaluate all points/theories/studies referred to. Your response should be in the form of an essay with a clear introduction and conclusion.

You should spend approximately 45 minutes answering this part of the question.

Class

Key concepts

This recap activity will ensure that you go over those all-important key concepts. Complete the key concept chart by writing a definition of the concept and where possible include which sociologist uses it. Refer to your core textbook or your classroom notes.

Key concepts	Definitions
Social class	
NS-SEC	
Bourgeoisie	
Proletariat	
Market situation	
Work situation	
Social mobility	
Old boy network	
Knowledge class	
Super-rich	
Middle class	
White-collar workers	
Social exclusion	

Mix and match

The purpose of this exercise is to test your knowledge of key pieces of sociological research within the topic of social class. You will need to match the explanation of the research with the name of the sociologist. Each sociologist is numbered and the explanation of study is lettered. Match the correct explanation with the sociologist by writing the correct letter in the blank box provided. Then check at the bottom of the page to see if you have matched the two correctly.

Sociologist

1 Sorenson (2000) ☐

2 Scott (1991) ☐

3 Braverman (1974) ☐

4 Marsland (1996) ☐

5 Davis and Moore (1945) ☐

6 Jones (1997) ☐

7 Goldthorpe (1968) ☐

Research/theory

A
Pay is related to talent. The most functionally important jobs are given to the most talented individuals who are paid the highest wages as a reward.

B
The proletariat no longer sell their labour to the bourgeoisie. They now 'rent it out'. This means wages can fluctuate according to the skills of the worker and the economic climate.

C
The welfare state makes the underclass dependent and they are therefore less able to support themselves.

D
The term 'ghetto poor' are those disadvantaged by both their social class and their race who are poor through no fault of their own.

E
Many white-collar jobs in the capitalist economy are going through a process of 'deskilling' where specialist knowledge becomes replaced with machines and automation.

F
Research into manual workers in Luton showed that the identity of the working class was changing. They had an instrumental attitude to work and increasingly privatised lifestyles.

G
The upper class maintain their position in society through operating social closure and taking part in the old boy network. This ensures that the high status jobs are given to other upper-class people.

Check your knowledge quick fire quiz

This multiple choice quiz will test your knowledge on the topic of social class. Each question will be worth a number of points; the points are indicated at the end of the question. The more points a question is worth, the more difficult it is: the top mark questions reflect whether you have read your core textbook thoroughly. Once you have ticked the answer you believe to be correct, add up your score to reveal whether you are a class expert!

1 *The National Statistics Socio-Economic Classification (NS-SEC) measures class according to what?* **(2 points)**

a) ☐ Income

b) ☐ Value of assets

c) ☐ Occupation

2 *The difference between the percentage of pupils from managerial backgrounds and the percentage of pupils from unskilled manual backgrounds achieving 5 GCSEs A*–C was what?* **(3 points)**

a) ☐ 45 per cent

b) ☐ 77 per cent

c) ☐ 32 per cent

3 *The term 'polarisation' means:* **(3 points)**

a) ☐ The gap between rich and poor is narrowing

b) ☐ The gap between rich and poor is getting wider

c) ☐ It is too simplistic to talk about 'rich' and 'poor'

4 *The term '30/30/40 society' was used by who?* **(4 points)**

a) ☐ Mount (2004)

b) ☐ Dahrendorf (1987)

c) ☐ Hutton (1995)

5 *Which view of the underclass does Murray (1990) provide?* **(3 points)**

a) ☐ Cultural

b) ☐ Functionalist

c) ☐ Structural

6 *Who argues that there is a clear division within the middle class between those who work in the public sector and those who are private sector entrepreneurs?* **(3 points)**

a) ☐ Savage et al. (1992)

b) ☐ Goldthorpe (1968)

c) ☐ Willis (1977)

7 *Which of the following is not part of the 'tri level class structure'?* **(2 points)**

a) ☐ Upper class

b) ☐ Working class

c) ☐ Underclass

Possible 20 points

17–20 Well done! You are a class expert!

12–16 It's official: you are on your way to becoming a 'sociology star'!

7–11 Looks like you might be avoiding the more difficult questions – get back to reading that textbook!

0–6 Oh dear, you're not going to win any 'sociology student of the year' prizes!

Answers: 1. c, 2. a, 3. b, 4. c, 5. a, 6. a, 7. c

Theory identifier

The statements below reflect the viewpoints of one of the following theories: functionalism, Marxism, neo-Marxism, Weberianism, feminism or postmodernism. Identify which theory goes with which statement by writing in the space above the statement.

1 _____

Social class is made up of people who share the same market situation and work situation.

2 _____

Class is dead. Divisions based on social class are no longer important as people no longer see themselves in class terms.

3 _____

In capitalist economies the bourgeoisie control and exploit the proletariat in the pursuit of profit.

4 _____

The middle class are a permanent feature of contemporary capitalist societies and they hold a position as both the exploited and exploiters.

5 _____

Social class inequalities are inevitable features of healthy societies where talent and hard work are rewarded. Those who are talented and work hard will secure a position which is higher in the class structure.

6 _____

Women are more disadvantaged in a capitalist economy than men are. This is because they work unpaid doing housework and childcare and also because they are paid less than men on average. They are therefore more likely to hold a lower-class position.

7 _____

Those who work in non-manual employment generally have a higher status position in society than those who do not. This will lead society to become more fragmented and polarised.

Class

Applying research studies task

The following is a list of some of the key concepts you may need to refer to when answering questions on the class topic. Fill in the spaces in the adjacent column with details of a sociologist and their research which could be used to illustrate each concept. The first one is done for you. Answers can be found at the back of the book.

Key concepts	Sociologist/research
Consumption	Pakulski and Waters (1996) argue that today people buy the identities they want through consumption rather than basing their identities on their social class.
Meritocracy	
Deskilling	
Ideological state apparatus	
Contradictory class position	
Embourgeoisement	
Cultural reproduction	
Proletarianisation	
Underclass	

ExamCafé

Exploring social inequality and difference: class

Exam answer-based activity

The answers below are examples of well-written responses to two G674 social class questions. Your task is to match the examiner's comments listed at the bottom with the numbers listed in the bodies of the exam answers. You must match the lettered examiner comments with the numbered points. You can then check at the end of the examiner comments to see if you are correct. The purpose of this activity is to give you an awareness of the key points which are required to answer these questions and of where the skills of AO1, AO2a and AO2b are being used.

Question 3 / 4 (a)
Outline the evidence that the working class are disadvantaged in society. (20 marks)

Student answer

It would appear that in the contemporary UK the working class are disadvantaged in areas such as education, the criminal justice system and health.

Education statistics show that the working class suffer a disadvantage in terms of both educational achievement and participation in further and higher education. In 2002, 77 per cent of students from managerial or professional backgrounds had achieved 5 GCSEs grades A*-C, compared with only 32 per cent of those from unskilled manual backgrounds. **1** ☐

Several possible explanations have been offered for this. Smith and Noble claim that material factors are to blame. Working-class families are not able to afford additional educational resources and also working-class children may miss more school due to poorer health and diet. Douglas, on the other hand, suggests that working-class parents take less interest in their children's education and are less likely to attend parents' evenings.

Those from lower social classes are less likely to participate in further and higher education and less likely to attend the most prestigious universities. Forsythe and Furlong argue that this is partly due to the prospect of debt and delay in earnings which continuing in education would mean. It has also been suggested that universities are middle-class environments and working-class students find this intimidating due to both a lack of culture capital and a lack of familiarity with the experience. **2** ☐

Health is another area where the working class suffer a disadvantage. Evidence from the Healthcare Commission shows that the lower social classes have a lower life expectancy. In 1997-99 men in the highest social class would live 7.4 years longer than men in the lowest social class. Those who work in routine occupations have the worst self-reported health and are more likely to suffer illness or injury associated with the workplace. These findings were also supported by Shaw and Davey Smith who compared poor and affluent areas of the UK between 1992 and 2003. They found that health inequality was increasing.

In terms of crime it could also be argued that the working class suffer a disadvantage. According to Home Office statistics working-class males are more likely to be stopped and searched by police, arrested and sent to prison. Serious and repeat offenders are disproportionately from the lowest social classes and 41 per cent of the prison population are from the lowest social classes. It is argued by some that this is because they commit more crime. Lea and Young claim that the working class commit more crime because of relative deprivation and marginalisation. However, others argue that they are more likely to be targeted by the police. Becker suggests that due to policing practices the working class are more likely to be caught and labelled as deviant. Marxist sociologists agree and claim that the middle class get away with crime in the form of corporate and white-collar crime. **3** ☐

Examiner comments

a) Good knowledge of three different areas well supported with evidence. The candidate could have added further breadth to this answer by referring to a fourth topic area. (AO1 and AO2a)

b) Effective use of statistical evidence. However, not all sources are referred to. (AO1)

c) Some use of concepts such as 'culture capital'. However, further concepts could have been included. (AO1)

Now try your own

Now try to write an answer to the question below. It is a good idea to try writing exam answers under timed conditions. You should spend 20 minutes writing your answer.

◆ Outline the evidence that the upper class are at an advantage in our society. (20 marks)

Question 3 / 4 (b)
Assess Marxist explanations of social class. (40 marks)

Student answer

Marxist explanations of social class focus on two main classes: the bourgeoisie and the proletariat. They believe that within capitalist societies the proletariat are exploited for their labour power by the bourgeoisie. This relationship leads to inequality within society and leads to the proletariat being disadvantaged in many aspects of life. This essay will explore and assess the Marxist explanation and compare this with alternative explanations of social class.

Marx argued that the ruling class, the bourgeoisie, owned the means of production. They are in a position of power as they are able to both control the price at which they sell the goods and the wages they pay those who work for them. By selling the goods for more and paying the workers less the ruling class are able to make large profits and give themselves wealth and power. Marx claimed that they then used this wealth and power to control all other aspects of society. Those who work for them, the proletariat, are dependent on the ruling class to provide them with jobs and wages. Marx believed that the ruling class used other institutions in society to convey the message that society was fair so that the ruling class were able to maintain their power. For example, through education the proletariat are taught that if they work hard they can achieve better jobs with higher pay. This leads the workers to work hard and conform in the hope that one day they will be better off too. Marx argued that one day this class system would be overturned when the workers staged a revolution and overthrew capitalism. He thought this would lead to the introduction of a fairer, communist economic system.

Marx's theory has been criticised as this revolution did not happen. However, the theory still holds some relevance for today's society. For example, the majority of the UK's wealth is still owned by a minority of the population. In 2002, the richest 1 per cent of the UK population owned 23 per cent of the nation's wealth. The higher classes also benefit from better educational achievements, better health, and jobs with better pay and working conditions. **1** ☐

However, in other ways the theory lacks relevance today. The idea that a system of only two classes exists does not apply. It doesn't account for the complexities of our class system and the existence of the middle class which is both the largest class and the fastest growing.

Neo-Marxist sociologists, on the other hand, have attempted to explain and include this class group. Theorists such as Wright have explained the middle class in terms of their 'contradictory class location'. The middle class are both able to exploit the working class and be exploited by the upper class. He claims that the middle class are a permanent feature of the class structure. Wright concluded that class conflict and exploitation are more complicated than Marx suggested but are still the basis of power and wealth in society. **2** ☐

Weber, alternatively, proposed an explanation of class which looks in more detail at peoples' occupational situation. **3** ☐ He proposed that it was too simplistic to look solely at peoples' relationship to the means of production and suggests that we should also consider their work and market situations. A person's market situation comes from the amount of money they receive (their income), while their work situation is related to the conditions of service they receive in their job (e.g. hours, perks, pension, etc.). Weber claimed that the higher a person's skills, talents and qualifications, the better their work and market situation. Weber believed that class positions were a lot less fixed than Marx suggested and that social mobility was a feature of contemporary life. **4** ☐

However, postmodern sociologists such as Pakulski and Waters argue that class and social mobility are no longer important in contemporary society. **5** ☐ They even go as far as to say that class is dead. They argue that we live in an individualised society where people no longer see themselves in class terms. Consumption means that people buy into the image and an identity they want rather than this being based on their job or occupational status. However, Pakulski and Waters have been criticised for having little empirical evidence to support their claims.

It is evident that although Marxist explanations of class have been very important in providing one of the first and most influential analyses, they do not explain all the changes which have occurred in contemporary society. These explanations have also been criticised for only considering class background in isolation without also considering gender, ethnicity or age as dimensions of inequality. **6** ☐

Examiner comments

a) Effective use of contemporary examples to illustrate points made, for example, in linking recent statistics on income and wealth to the Marxist theory. This will gain the candidate marks for knowledge and understanding. (AO1)

b) New paragraph clearly links back to the question asked, illustrating that the candidate has both understood the question and is clearly answering it. This will give marks for interpretation and application. (AO2a)

c) The candidate shows knowledge of a range of theories. However, they could also consider functionalist explanations of class in comparison. This would give further marks for knowledge and understanding (AO1) as well as providing an opportunity for evaluation. (AO2b)

d) The candidate effectively combines a knowledge of both theory and research evidence, for example, in linking Pakulski and Waters to the postmodernist theory. This provides further marks for knowledge and understanding. (AO1)

e) Some effective use of analysis and evaluation. The candidate could develop this through ensuring all theories are clearly evaluated and through introducing some counter evaluation. Providing an evaluation of the Weberian theory would give further marks for analysis and evaluation. (AO2b)

f) The candidate uses a range of key concepts throughout the answer, for example, 'contradictory class location'. These are also linked to specific theories and sociologists. This will also provide marks for knowledge and understanding. (AO1)

Answers: 1.a, 2.f, 3.b, 4.e, 5.d, 6.c

Now try your own

Now try to write answers to the questions below. It is a good idea to try writing exam answers under timed conditions. You should spend 45 minutes writing each answer.

- ◆ Assess sociological explanations of social class inequality. (40 marks)

- ◆ Assess sociological explanations of changes to the class structure. (40 marks)

Gender

Key concepts

This recap activity will ensure that you go over those all-important key concepts. Complete the key concept chart by writing a definition of the concept and, where possible, include which sociologist uses it. Refer to your core textbook or your classroom notes.

Key concepts	Definitions
Gender	
Inequality	
Feminism	
Patriarchy	
Pay gap	
Glass ceiling	
Horizontal segregation	
Vertical segregation	
Capitalism	
Second wave feminism	
Post-feminism	

Mix and match

The purpose of this exercise is to test your knowledge of key pieces of sociological research within the topic of gender. You will need to match the explanation of the research with the name of the sociologist. Each sociologist is numbered and the explanation of study is lettered. Match the correct explanation with the sociologist by writing the correct letter in the blank box provided. Then check at the bottom of the page to see if you have matched the two correctly.

Sociologist

1 Friedan (1963) ☐

2 Walby (1990) ☐

3 Hakim (2000) ☐

4 Hartmann (1981) ☐

5 Firestone (1971) ☐

Research/theory

A
The source of patriarchy lies in biological differences. Women's ability to give birth results in dominance by men.

B
Women exercise choice in relation to their position at home and in the workplace. The choices they make may disadvantage them.

C
Patriarchy is not one overarching system but instead operates though different institutions, e.g. the media and education.

D
Gender inequality is a result of both patriarchy and economic factors. You can only explain gender inequality by considering both of these.

E
Gender inequality is a product of general inequality in society which has been allowed to proceed unchallenged for centuries. The solution is to remove barriers blocking equality.

Check your knowledge quick fire quiz

This multiple choice quiz will test your knowledge on the topic of gender. Each question will be worth a number of points; the points are indicated at the end of the question. The more points a question is worth, the more difficult it is: the top mark questions reflect whether you have read your core textbook thoroughly. Once you have ticked the answer you believe to be correct, add up your score to reveal whether you are a gender expert!

I *Which piece of legislation made it illegal to pay men and women different rates for the same job?*
(2 points)

a) ☐ Sex Discrimination Act 1975

b) ☐ Sexism Act 1990

c) ☐ Equal Pay Act 1970

2 *The following statement is a criticism of which sociological theory? 'It is not clear whether the theory is blaming capitalism or patriarchy for gender inequalities.'* **(3 points)**

a) ☐ Radical feminism

b) ☐ Marxist feminism

c) ☐ Liberal feminism

3 *Which of the following terms is used to describe the way males and females are concentrated in different sectors of work?* **(3 points)**

a) ☐ Horizontal segregation

b) ☐ Vertical segregation

c) ☐ Glass ceiling

4 *According to the Cranfield Institute's report in 2007, what number of females made up new appointments as directors to FTSE 100 companies?* **(4 points)**

a) ☐ 30

b) ☐ 152

c) ☐ 70

5 *Which of the following is not a group of women identified by Catherine Hakim in her preference theory?* **(3 points)**

a) ☐ Work centred

b) ☐ Adaptive

c) ☐ Children centred

6 *Who argues that patriarchy is not universal and instead operates in different ways in different places?* **(3 points)**

a) ☐ Benston

b) ☐ Barron and Norris

c) ☐ Walby

7 *Which of the following is not a feminist sociologist?* **(2 points)**

a) ☐ Parsons

b) ☐ Firestone

c) ☐ Walters

Possible 20 points

17–20 Well done! You are a gender expert!

12–16 It's official: you are on your way to becoming a 'sociology star'

7–11 Looks like you might be avoiding the more difficult questions – get back to reading that textbook!

0–6 Oh dear, you're not going to win any 'sociology student of the year' prizes!

Answers: 1. c, 2. b, 3. a, 4. a, 5. c, 6. c, 7. a

Theory identifier

The statements below reflect the viewpoints of one of the following theories:
liberal feminism, Marxist feminism, radical feminism, black feminism, post-feminism,
functionalism or Weberianism. Identify which theory goes with which statement
by writing in the space above the statement.

1 _____

Men and women naturally serve different social roles. These differences are ascribed at birth and contribute
to a healthy, smooth running society.

2 _____

Gender inequalities are a result of socialisation and have been unchallenged for centuries. Equal opportunities
legislation can play a vital role in removing inequalities.

3 _____

Women are more likely than men to be found in the secondary labour market. The secondary labour market
includes jobs which are lower paid, insecure and have poor promotion prospects.

4 _____

White middle-class feminists have ignored the experiences of ethnic minority women and the additional
disadvantage they face.

5 _____

Women have choices and the choices they make may lead to disadvantage. For example, women who have
children may choose to work part time and this could lead to the perception that they are not committed
workers.

6 _____

Women are more disadvantaged in a capitalist economy than men are. This is because they work unpaid
doing housework and childcare and also because they are paid less than men on average.

7 _____

Patriarchy is the cause of women's oppression. Men control and dominate all aspects of social life.

Answers: 1. functionalism, 2. liberal feminism, 3. Weberianism,
4. black feminism, 5. post-feminism, 6. Marxist feminism, 7. radical feminism

Applying research studies task

The following is a list of some of the key concepts you may need to refer to when answering questions on the gender topic. Fill in the spaces in the adjacent column with details of a sociologist and their research which could be used to illustrate each concept. The first one is done for you. Answers can be found at the back of the book.

Key concepts	Sociologist/research
Dual labour market	Barron and Norris (1976) argue that there are two markets: primary and secondary. Women are likely to be found in the secondary labour market where jobs are lower paid, insecure and have fewer promotion prospects.
Reserve army of labour	
Dual systems theory	
Preference theory	
Patriarchy	
Positive discrimination	
Expressive roles	
Instrumental roles	

ExamCafé

Exploring social inequality and difference: gender

Exam answer-based activity

The answer below is an example of a well-written response to a G674 gender question. Your task is to match the examiner's comments listed at the bottom with the numbers listed in the body of the exam answer. You must match the lettered examiner comments with the numbered points. You can then check at the bottom of the page to see if you are correct. The purpose of this activity is to give you an awareness of the key points which are required to answer this question and of where the skills of AO1, AO2a and AO2B are being used.

Question 3 / 4 (a)
Outline the evidence that women are disadvantaged in society. (20 marks)

Student answer

It would seem that most women in the contemporary UK are disadvantaged in areas such as work, education, poverty and the family. Women are drastically disadvantaged in the labour market. Based on full-time employment statistics, there is a clear pay gap with women earning on average £394 a week and men £496 (ONS, 2007). **1** ☐

Furthermore, vertical segregation often takes place, meaning that men often hold the positions of higher status which women are prevented from achieving because of the 'glass ceiling'. Only 11 per cent of women are managers and senior post-holders compared with 18 per cent of men. Women are also less likely to be employed than men with 70 per cent of working-age women in work compared with 79 per cent of working-age men (ONS). **2** ☐

Women would also seem to be disadvantaged in some areas of education, particularly regarding subject choice. Anne Colley stated that certain subjects still have a gendered character which is influenced by cultural characteristics of masculinity and femininity. Males predominantly choose subjects such as engineering, business and physics while girls predominantly choose the humanities or 'caring' subjects. The gap becomes wider as they reach further education. This would seem to imply that girls are disadvantaged because of the restricted subject choices they make. This may lead to horizontal segregation, with women following careers such as nursing and childcare which are lower paid and lower status. **3** ☐

Women are more likely to live in poverty than men and spend longer periods in unemployment (Berthoud, 2002). Berthoud stated that this was because of:

- Labour market disadvantage, where women are more likely to be employed in lower paid, lower skilled and less secure jobs.

- Their primary care role. Women are still viewed as the primary carers of children which can have an adverse effect on their employment which often follows an M-shaped pattern.

- Demographic changes. There has been an increase in the number of lone-parent families headed by the mother. These tend to earn less than two-carer families and the lone female carer may have fewer skills which can hinder their job opportunities. They may have poorer health and live in less prosperous areas with fewer job opportunities available.

Finally, women are often disadvantaged within the family. As they are seen as the primary carers of children, they often have to carry out the majority of domestic tasks or, as Walby states, be subject to 'private patriarchy'. Muslim women are more likely to be constrained by family life and be subjected to 'private patriarchy'. Seager (1997) found that women spent much more time each on domestic tasks than men and that men had more leisure and rest time than women. Duncombe and Marsden argue that women often do a 'triple shift' of paid work, emotion work and housework/childcare. **4** ☐

Examiner comments

a) Wide-ranging synoptic knowledge and understanding shown by referring to four different areas. (AO1)

b) Excellent use of key concepts such as 'glass ceiling'. (AO1)

c) Answer is well introduced with clear and relevant statistics. Date and source of statistics is stated. (AO1)

d) Effective links are made between topics, for example the link between educational subject choices and future careers/earnings. (AO1)

Now try your own

Now try to write an answer to the question below. It is a good idea to try writing exam answers under timed conditions. You should spend 20 minutes writing your answer.

◆ Outline the evidence that males are disadvantaged in society. (20 marks)

Question 3 /4 (b)
Assess feminist explanations of gender inequality in the workplace. (40 marks)

rewind

Student answer

There is little doubt about the existence of gender inequality in the workplace, with women being the victims. Women earn far less than men. Based on full-time employment statistics, there is a clear pay gap with women earning on average £394 a week and men £496 (ONS, 2007). **1** ☐ Furthermore, women are often prevented from achieving the top positions in management because of the 'glass ceiling' leading to 'vertical segregation'. Eleven per cent of women are managers and senior post-holders compared with 18 per cent of men. There are a number of feminist views which have identified reasons for this inequality and this essay will attempt to address them all.

Radical feminists argue that there is a basic conflict between all men and women. Because society is patriarchal it leads to men being able to exploit and oppress women to their disadvantage in the labour market. Stanko argues that men use sexual harassment to intimidate women who seek to enter into areas of traditionally male employment. In jobs predominantly done by women, they are expected to look sexually attractive and accept that they may receive unwanted male attention. However, Stanko looks at only one source of inequality in the workplace and ignores others such as ethnicity. Furthermore, she pays little attention to the operation of the labour market as a whole. Pringle, also a radical feminist, argues that the work of female secretaries is largely governed by the patriarchal images of the job, thus it is hard for secretaries to be taken seriously or have their skills valued because of these images. They are often viewed as extensions to their employers, making it hard for them to be valued in their own right and to achieve promotion to management posts. However, Pringle provides no empirical evidence to support her claims and her argument could be seen as a generalisation of how secretaries are viewed. **2** ☐

Marxist feminists offer a different perspective in arguing that gender inequalities in the workplace are a result of capitalism, which exploits them. **3** ☐ Braverman states that women have been drawn into the lower paid areas of work such as the service sector. Changes in the labour market have led to an increased demand for part-time unskilled workers and women have been seen as suitable for these positions. However, not all working women are in unskilled jobs. Beechy stated that jobs such as nursing require high levels of skill and qualifications but are subject to low rates of pay and low status as they are viewed as women's work. Beechy described women as a 'reserve army of labour'. **4** ☐ They are a group of unemployed individuals who are looking for work and are willing to work part-time. This works to the advantage of capitalism as the employers can keep wages low knowing that there will always be workers willing to take the jobs on offer. Thus gender inequalities in the workplace are able to continue. However, 70 per cent of working-age women are in employment compared with 79 per cent of working-age men so the gap is not that big.

Socialist feminists bring together the ideas of Marxist and radical feminists. They argue that women are exploited by both patriarchy and capitalism. This is also known as the 'dual systems theory', indicating that women are exploited both at home and at work. However, other feminists have criticised socialist feminists for not making it clear how patriarchy and capitalism work together to create inequality for women in the workplace.

Alternatively, black feminists have criticised the views of radical, Marxist and socialist feminists for failing to look at the effect that racism can have on women. Yuval-Davies argues that other feminists have 'forgotten' to look at ethnicity as their theories are ethnocentric, focusing on the experiences of white women and not acknowledging that the experiences of black women may be different. She describes black women as being 'doubly disadvantaged'. **5** ☐ However, Walby argued that women were exploited by the three systems of patriarchy, capitalism and racism, showing that ethnicity had not been forgotten.

Weberians provide an alternative to the feminist arguments. They point to the 'dual labour market' theory which illustrates gender inequality in the workplace. The primary labour market has jobs which are highly paid with high status, good working conditions and good promotion prospects. The secondary labour market has jobs which are low paid, insecure and with poor conditions of service. Weberians argue that while both men and women are found in the secondary labour market, there are fewer women in the primary labour market. Women are seen as having less interest in careers, promotion and higher wages, meaning that their position in the labour market is stagnant. Beechey argues, however, that many women are found in the primary labour market in jobs such as teaching, nursing and social care. This theory only really explains the differences within the manufacturing sector.

Liberal feminists offer yet another explanation and suggest that gender role socialisation is responsible for reproducing gender inequalities in the workplace. They believe this leads to the sexual division of labour where masculinity is seen as dominant and femininity subordinate. Anne Oakley stated that women do less well in the labour market as a result of the dominance of the mother-housewife role. Women are taught to believe that they should work part time because of their responsibilities as wives and mothers. This leads to male dominance within the labour market. A more contemporary explanation for the pay gap is that women are less likely than men to ask for a pay rise. This also may be due to socialisation.

However, post-feminists take a different approach in explaining gender inequalities. Hakim argues that gender inequalities in the workplace, such as the pay gap, are not due to structural factors, e.g. capitalism or patriarchy, but due to the rational choices that women make and their 'preferences'. For example, women make the choice to have children and to work part time and these choices may lead them to not take their careers as seriously as men do. Other feminists have criticised Hakim for twisting the data to suit her arguments. They challenge the statements she makes concerning cultural choices and state that the pay gap cannot be explained as simply as this.

Finally, postmodernists argue that patriarchy and inequality can no longer be explained in terms of gender. Women are too divided by age, class and ethnicity to be able to draw clear conclusions. Women's experience in the labour market will vary dramatically depending on the type of work they do. However, there is still a clear difference in the average pay between men and women. Furthermore, in 2004 the Fawcett Society found that only 5 out of 43 police chief constables were women and only 1 out of 12 judges in the House of Lords was a woman, which highlights the inequality that exists. **6** ☐

In conclusion, as mentioned at the start, women do experience inequality at work but it is hard to lay the blame solely at one doorstep. Clearly the pay gap in our society could be due to the capitalist and patriarchal society we live in, as the radical and Marxist feminists argue. However, there is also evidence that inequality is due to the cultural choices that women make, as Hakim's 'preference theory' claims. It is an intriguing debate which will no doubt continue for a long time.

a) Effective use of contemporary examples to illustrate points made. This will gain the candidate marks for knowledge and understanding. (AO1)

b) New paragraphs clearly link back to the question asked, illustrating that the candidate has both understood the question and is clearly answering it. This will give marks for interpretation and application. (AO2a)

c) Effective use of statistics to set the scene for the question. These are supported with both the date and the source. This will give the candidate marks for knowledge and understanding. (AO1)

d) The candidate effectively combines a knowledge of both theory and research evidence which provides further marks for knowledge and understanding. (AO1)

e) Highly effective use of analysis and evaluation. The candidate not only makes evaluative points but also counter evaluates these. This provides marks for analysis and evaluation. (AO2b)

f) The candidate uses a range of key concepts throughout the answer. These are also linked to specific theories and sociologists. This also will provide marks for knowledge and understanding. (AO1)

Now try your own

Now try to write an answer to the question below. It is a good idea to try writing exam answers under timed conditions. You should spend 45 minutes writing your answer.

◆ Assess sociological explanations of gender inequality. (40 marks)

Ethnicity

Key concepts

This recap activity will ensure that you go over those all-important key concepts. Complete the key concept chart by writing a definition of the concept and, where possible, include which sociologist uses it. Refer to your core textbook or your classroom notes.

Key concepts	Definitions
Ethnicity	
Race	
Super-diversity	
Ethnocentric	
Institutional racism	
Ethnic penalty	
Assimilation	
Racialised	
Islamophobia	

Mix and match

The purpose of this exercise is to test your knowledge of some of the key pieces of sociological research on ethnicity. You will need to match the explanation of the research/theory with the name of the sociologist/title of the study. Each sociologist/title of study is numbered and the explanation of the research/theory is lettered. Identify the correct explanations by writing the correct letters in the blank boxes provided. Then check at the bottom of the page to see if you have matched them correctly.

Sociologist/title of study

1 Ginn and Arber (2001) ☐

2 Ethnocentric curriculum ☐

3 Runnymede Trust (1997) ☐

4 Berthoud and Modood (1997) ☐

5 'Super-diversity' ☐

Research/theory

A
This term is used by Verotec (2007) to describe the heterogeneous nature of the new immigrants.

B
This report identified four aspects of cultural racism towards Muslims and Islam.

C
These two sociologists carried out an analysis of household income based on the findings of the fourth Policy Studies Institute (PSI) and found that Pakistani and Bangladeshi households are more likely than other ethnic groups to experience poverty.

D
The research carried out by these two sociologists found that ethnic minority groups, especially women, are disproportionally dependent on state pensions later on in life.

E
This term is used to explain why some ethnic groups adopt anti-school and anti-education cultures. Pupils from ethnic groups can feel either ignored or marginalised by the national curriculum.

Check your knowledge quick fire quiz

This multiple choice quiz will test your knowledge on the topic of ethnicity. Each question will be worth a number of points; the points are indicated at the end of the question. The more points a question is worth, the more difficult it is: the top mark questions reflect whether you have read your core textbook thoroughly. Once you have ticked the answer you believe to be correct, add up your score to reveal whether you are an ethnicity expert!

1 *What sociologist distinguished between racial prejudice and racial discrimination, and argued that racial discrimination is based on action and goes beyond racist thoughts?* **(3 points)**

a) ☐ Cashmore (1984)

b) ☐ Hall (1982)

c) ☐ Berthoud (1997)

2 *What is the term used to define the disadvantage that ethnic minorities experience in the labour market, compared with their British white counterparts?* **(4 points)**

a) ☐ Outsider penalty

b) ☐ Racial penalty

c) ☐ Ethnic penalty

3 *In reaction to the discrimination experienced by many ethnic minorities in the workplace, what did Mason (2003) find they prominently figured in?* **(3 points)**

a) ☐ Entrepreneurial activity

b) ☐ Manufacturing activity

c) ☐ Web-based activity

4 *Evidence from 'Business in the Community' found that South Asian minority groups are being dubbed which new social class group?* **(3 points)**

a) ☐ 'new underclass'

b) ☐ 'new middle class'

c) ☐ 'new working class'

5 *Which two sociologists found in their study on social mobility that second-generation immigrants may have gained from the move to a service sector economy?* **(4 points)**

a) ☐ Cashmore and Troyna (1990)

b) ☐ Ginn and Arber (2001)

c) ☐ Iganski and Payne (1999)

Possible 17 points

13–17 Well done! You are an ethnicity expert!

8–12 It's official: you are becoming a 'sociology star'!

4–7 Looks like you might be avoiding the more difficult questions – get back to reading that textbook!

0–3 Oh dear, you're not going to win any 'sociology student of the year' prizes!

Unit 4: Exploring social inequality and difference

Answers: 1.a, 2.c, 3.a, 4.b, 5.c

Theory identifier

The statements below reflect the viewpoints of one of the following theories:
Marxism, neo-Marxism, functionalism, Weberianism or postmodernism.
Identify which theory goes with which statement by writing in the space above
the statement.

1 _____

Cox 1948 is one of the earliest writers of this theory on racial difference. Cox believes that racism has
helped to maintain a false class consciousness by using a divide-and-rule tactic.

2 _____

This theory argues that in order to maintain social order, minority groups slowly adapt to the majority
culture over time: this process is known as assimilation.

3 _____

Rex and Moore (1967) argue that minority groups are placed in the secondary part of the dual labour
market. Life chances, status and the market position of those in the secondary labour market are inferior
to those in the primary labour market.

4 _____

This theory is concerned with seeking to ensure that grand themes and analysis are no longer applied to
the study of ethnic groups. They argue that future studies on ethnic groups should consider the super-diversity
of ethnic groups and that they should not be seen as a homogenous group.

5 _____

S. Hall (1999), a supporter of the theory, argues that ethnic minorities have been used as scapegoats by the
media which is part of the ideological stage apparatus. In the 1970s Hall claimed the media diverted attention
away from the recession by focusing on immigration.

Applying research studies task

The following is a list of some of the key concepts you may need to refer to when answering questions on ethnic inequality. Fill in the spaces in the adjacent column with details of a sociologist/theorist and their research/theory, or a description of the concept, which could be used to illustrate each concept. The first one is done for you. Answers can be found at the back of the book.

Key concepts	Sociologist/research/theory
Institutional racism	Can be intentional or unintentional: both have a similar effect. When applied to institutions such as the police, it can manifest itself in the norms, values and belief systems of the institution.
'Negatively privileged status groups'	
'American negro'	
'Divide-and-rule tactic'	
Intentional racism	

ExamCafé

Exploring social inequality and difference: ethnicity

Exam answer-based activity

The answer below is an example of a well-written response to a G674 ethnicity question. Your task is to match the examiner's comments listed at the bottom with the numbers listed in the body of the exam answer. You must match the lettered examiner comments with the numbered points. You can then check at the bottom of the page to see if you are correct. The purpose of this activity is to give you an awareness of the key points which are required to answer this question and of where the skills of AO1, AO2a and AO2b are being used.

Question 3 / 4 (a)
Outline the evidence that ethnic inequalities still exist in the contemporary UK. (20 marks)

Student answer

The inequalities experienced by ethnic minorities are something that has interested both British and American sociologists, although British sociologists are more likely to use the term 'ethnic difference' whereas their American counterparts tend to use the concept of 'race'. Miles, a neo-Marxist, in his theory 'Racialised class fractions' argues that we should dispense with the term 'race' as it is used as a term to divide people, particularly the working class. It creates inter-class conflict with the white working class viewing ethnic minorities as a threat; capitalists use this to their advantage and prosper on the racialised class fractions that exist within the working class. Furthermore, Miles argues that ethnic minorities also experience differential treatment, even in the middle classes: they will never fully be accepted into the middle-class culture as they will be seen in terms of their 'race' first. It is argued that ethnic minorities experience inequalities in a number of areas, including education, the workplace and the media, and some ethnic minority groups are more likely to be living in poverty. The fourth Policy Studies Institute survey of 1997 gave an insight into the extent of poverty experienced by Pakistani and Bangladeshi households. Furthermore, Caribbean, Indian and African Asian households were more likely than their white counterparts to be living in relative poverty. The findings led Berthoud (1997) to name Pakistani and Bangladeshi households as among the social groups most likely to be living in poverty. **1** ☐

Inequalities for Pakistani and Bangladeshi households are also evident in the workplace. Evidence from the Business in the Community study found that 75 per cent of working-age Bangladeshi women and 69 per cent of working-age Pakistani women were not working or seeking employment, adding a gendered dimension to the inequalities experienced by those two ethnic groups. **2** ☐ However, the same study found that overall it was in fact black Caribbean males who had the highest unemployment rate of all ethnic groups. Mason (2003) argues that one of the main reasons why some ethnic groups experience an inferior labour market position is due to the attitudes of employers; this can lead to cultural racism. Cultural racism in the form of Islamophobia was identified in a report by the Runnymede Trust in 1997, which found that prejudice was evident in the media coverage of Muslim culture., discrimination in employment practices and an ethnocentric educational curriculum in compulsory education. **3** ☐

The Office for National Statistics supports these findings in its statistics on unemployment; Muslims, according to the ONS, are the most likely group to be employed in poorly paid and low-skilled jobs. **4** ☐

Neo-Weberians Rex and Moore (1967) help to explain how ethnic minorities become disadvantaged in the workplace through their dual labour market theory. They argue that many ethnic minorities are placed in the secondary part of the dual labour market, meaning that they generally occupy jobs which have a lower market situation and market position, which reduces the life chances of these individuals. Ethnic minorities also experience inequality from the other structures within society such as the mass media. In the 1970s and 1980s ethnic minorities, particularly young black males of Caribbean origin, were represented in the media as criminals and a threat to society. S. Hall (1978) argues that a moral panic was created by the media and then amplified by government and the police; Hall refers to this moral panic as 'the myth of black criminality'. The media exaggerated stories about young black males as perpetrators of muggings against white elderly victims; young black males were seen as 'folk devils' by the general public; the government and the police overacted to the situation; and 'Operation Swamp' was put into place by the Metropolitan Police. The police used an old Vagrancy Act from 1824, which became known as the 'Sus law'; this law allowed the police to stop and search any individual based on suspicion only that the individual may be about to commit a crime. The oppressive nature of the 'Sus law' led to the 1981 Brixton riots: young black males took an active form of resistance against the discrimination they had experienced from the authorities. **5** ☐

Since the riots of the 1980s and 1990s some steps have been taken to try and address some of the accusations of institutional racism which have been levelled at the Metropolitan Police. In 2000 the Race Relations Act was amended after the Macpherson Report on the death of Stephen Lawrence found that many public institutions were institutionally racist. The amended act meant that public institutions not only have to address unlawful discrimination when it happens, but they also have to be proactive in preventing it from occurring (Scottish Council for Voluntary Organisations website, April 2009). However, in 2004 the Criminal Justice System statistics found that even though black people made up only 2 per cent of the population, 14.6 per cent of stop and searches in England and Wales were on black people. **6** ☐

Although it is true to say that not all ethnic minorities experience the same level of inequalities, it is evident that inequalities are continuing to be experienced by certain ethnic groups.

Examiner comments

a) Good link into influence of other social characteristics in the experience of ethnic minorities and inequality. This part of the response would gain marks for AO1.

b) Good use of varied data in the explanation of cultural racism. This part of the response would gain marks for AO1 and AO2a.

c) Four areas of inequality identified and illustrated by the use of statistics on poverty. This part of the response would gain marks for AO1 and AO2a.

d) Again good link into another area, including relevant sociological evidence from the mass media section of the A2 syllabus. This part of the response would gain marks for AO1.

e) Links into education and ethnic inequality could have been developed.

f) Interesting facts but student could have made sure that statistics on stop and search findings were explicitly linked backed to the previous point made. This part of the response would have gained marks for AO1 and AO2a.

Now try your own

Now try to write answers to the questions below. It is a good idea to try writing these answers under timed conditions. You should spend approximately 20 minutes writing each answer.

◆ Outline the evidence that only some ethnic minority groups experience inequality in the contemporary UK. (20 marks)

◆ Outline the evidence that ethnic minorities experience greater disadvantages due to institutional racism. (20 marks)

Question 3 /4 (b)
Assess the sociological explanations of ethnic disadvantage in the contemporary UK. (40 marks)

rewind

Student answer

The view that ethnic disadvantage in the UK still exists in contemporary society will be discussed, assessed and evaluated by using structural, cultural and postmodern explanations. The structural explanations of neo-Marxism and neo-Weberianism support the idea that ethnic disadvantage is due to many situational constraints. The cultural explanation includes the host-immigrant model put forth by Patterson, and postmodern explanations stress that any explanation of ethnic disadvantage must consider the diversity of ethnic groups. This essay will draw from the different explanations identified to assess from a theoretical viewpoint whether ethnic disadvantage is as prominent today as it has been in the past. **1** ☐

The Office for National Statistics government website uses a classification scheme that identifies groups which share a common ethic background; schemes are very useful for monitoring purposes, with the positive intention of targeting areas of obvious ethnic disadvantage. However, such schemes have been accused of treating ethnic groups as one homogenous whole, when in fact the reality is they are considerably heterogeneous. For example, in the 2001 census Asians were grouped together under two main headings 'All Asian or Asian British' or 'Other Asian' (ONS, 2001). Such large groupings would not allow the government to target which ethnic groups within the Asian categories were being treated unfairly (Waugh et al., 2009). **2** ☐

Verotec (2007) goes on to develop this view by stating that there is now a far greater variety of groups and individuals living in the UK, from places around the world. He argues that there now exist relatively new and scattered groups of Romanians, Ghanaians, mainland Chinese, Afghans, Japanese, Kurds and many others. These ethnic groups will have a varied experience of disadvantage in the UK: in 2006 the Equality and Human Rights Commission found that there were noticeable differences in the employment rate for different ethnic groups; for white males 91 per cent were in full-time employment, whereas only 61 per cent of

Bangladeshi males were in full-time employment. Ginn and Arber 2001 argued that gender was also linked to ethnic disadvantage: they found that women from ethnic minority groups are disproportionately dependent on state pensions later in life, due to the fact that they earn less throughout their working life; they were unable to pay into a private pension. Marxists such as Castles and Kosack (1973) argue that ethnic minority groups and women are used as a reserve army of labour; they put forth three areas in which ethnic groups experience racial inequality: legitimatisation, divide-and-rule and scapegoating. Castles and Kosack argue that legitimatisation justifies the low pay and poor working conditions that the ethnic minorities experience; this is possibly due to the fact that they are seen as second-class citizens, and that they are exploited by the capitalists, who ensure that ethnic minorities are used as cheap labour. Secondly, they can divide and rule by dividing the working class between black and white. Employers use black and ethnic minorities as a reserve army of labour, preventing white workers from demanding higher wages by forcing the ethnic workers to work for lower wages than their white counterparts in order to survive. 3 ☐

However, Iganski and Payne (1999) would argue that the experience of second and third generation immigrants is not so bleak. Their study on social mobility suggested that while first generation immigrants were disadvantaged by the decline of the manufacturing economy, in fact second and third generation immigrants may have benefited from the move to the service sector and were able to prosper under the new service sector economy. Functionalist thinkers such as Patterson argued that the discrimination experienced by the first generation immigrants in the 1950s and 1960s was due to the cultural difference between the immigrants and the host community. He explains that Britain at the time had a homogenous culture in which there was a high degree of consensus over the norms and values of society; this consensus was disturbed by the arrival of immigrants who brought with them differing norms and values, from the types of food they ate to valuing different forms of religion. This led to social unrest and unintentional racism: the host community were trying to cope with the development of a culturally diverse society. 4 ☐

However, it was argued by Barker that the media was instrumental in stirring up racial hatred, with the printed media such as the tabloids representing ethnic minorities as a threat to social order. Van Dijk's (1991) study supports Barker's view. Van Dijk carried out content analysis of British newspapers during the period of the 1980s and found that there was a pattern, particularly from the tabloid press, of ethnic minorities being represented in a negative way, by being portrayed as either a threat through criminal behaviour or a threat in the form of representing something different from the norm, which should be resisted. A more recent study by Moore et al. in 2005 found similar stereotypes to Van Dijk, supporting the argument that ethnic minorities are still represented in a marginalised and negative way by the UK media. 5 ☐

Recently, Heath and Yi Cheung carried out statistical analysis to see if the concept of the 'ethnic penalty' still exists for ethnic minority groups. They found that for some ethnic minority groups there is in fact an 'ethnic penalty' and they concluded that certain ethnic groups such as Pakistani, Bangladeshi and Caribbean men and women were most likely to experience the 'ethnic penalty'. However, they did find that second and third generation immigrants were less likely to experience the 'ethnic penalty' than their first generation counterparts. Neo-Weberians such as Rex and Moore argue that minority groups were disadvantaged in the workplace because they formed part of the dual labour market, being placed in the secondary labour market, where they would occupy jobs which had limited chances of progression, low wages and came with a low status. To conclude, they found that their life chances and their market position were relatively poorer than their white counterparts. Postmodernists call for some caution as they argue that grand themes and analyses can no longer be applied to whole ethnic groups, as there is too much diversity. Modood supports this view by arguing that a more plural approach needs to be developed when considering ethnic relations; his work stresses the need for considering difference and diversity rather than commonality, and he believes that the view of ethnic minorities as victims is counterproductive. **6** ☐

Overall, the sociological explanations referred to would indicate that, even though there have been some changes in the life chances between first and subsequent generations of immigrants, there is still clear evidence that disadvantage for many ethnic minority groups still exists in the contemporary UK.

Examiner comments

a) Good evaluative comment on how the concept of ethnicity is operationalised. This part of the response would gain marks for AO1 and AO2b.

b) Good introduction, sets the scene with relevant theories referred to. This part of the response would gain marks for AO1.

c) Another alternative explanation included, although the postmodern analysis could have been developed. This part of the response would gain marks for AO1 and AO2b.

d) Good use of a prominent study of ethnic representation, followed up with a contemporary study. This part of the response would gain marks for AO1 and AO2a.

e) Good use of Marxist explanations of ethnic inequality. This part of the response would gain marks for AO1.

f) Alternative cultural explanation used to explain reasons for ethnic inequality, which adds another dimension to the debate. This part of the response would gain marks for AO1 and AO2b.

Now try your own

Now try to write answers to the questions below. It is a good idea to try writing these answers under timed conditions. You should spend 45 minutes writing each answer.

◆ Assess Weberian explanations of ethnic inequality in the contemporary UK. (40 marks)

◆ Assess the view that structural explanations of ethnic inequality are no longer relevant to the contemporary UK. (40 marks)

Age

Key concepts

This recap activity will ensure that you go over those all-important key concepts.
Complete the key concept chart by writing a definition of the concept and,
where possible, include which sociologist uses it. Refer to your core textbook
or your classroom notes.

Key concepts	Definitions
'Sandwich generation'	
Disengagement	
Glass ceiling	
Active ageing	
Demographic	
'Oldest old'	

Mix and match

The purpose of this exercise is to test your knowledge of some of the key pieces of sociological research on age. You will need to match the explanation of the research/theory with the name of the sociologist/title of the study. Each sociologist/title of study is numbered and the explanation of the research/theory is lettered. Identify the correct explanations by writing the correct letters in the blank boxes provided. Then check at the bottom of the page to see if you have matched them correctly.

Sociologist/title of study

1 Carrigan and Szmigin ☐

2 Milne and Harding (1999) ☐

3 'too old to employ' ☐

4 Featherstone and Hepworth (1999) ☐

5 Bytheway (1995) ☐

Research/theory

A
This sociologist argues that ageism is a misleading concept, as age is experienced differently in different sectors of society.

B
This phrase is applied to those who have experienced compulsory early retirement.

C
These postmodernists highlight that individual life-courses are heavily fragmented; therefore it is difficult to identify clear patterns of age-related behaviour in the workplace.

D
These two sociologists researched the lifestyles of over 1000 older people and found that two worlds existed. The first included those involved in 'active ageing'; the second, made up of people aged 80 years and over, lived alone and on a limited income.

E
These two sociologists have found in their studies that the media is responsible for marginalising the representation of older people by portraying them as decrepit and withering.

Answers: 1.E, 2.D, 3.B, 4.C, 5.A

Check your knowledge quick fire quiz

This multiple choice quiz will test your knowledge on the topic of age. Each question will be worth a number of points; the points are indicated at the end of the question. The more points a question is worth, the more difficult it is: the top mark questions reflect whether you have read your core textbook thoroughly. Once you have ticked the answer you believe to be correct, add up your score to reveal whether you are an age expert!

1 *In what year did legislation pass which makes it illegal for age discrimination to take place?* **(3 points)**

a) ☐ 2006

b) ☐ 2008

c) ☐ 2002

2 *In the 2002 MORI survey, what was the percentage of those who believed they had experienced discrimination in the form of ageism?* **(4 points)**

a) ☐ 50 per cent

b) ☐ 48 per cent

c) ☐ 38 per cent

3 *Which sociologist argues that old age is culturally experienced differently by different people?* **(3 points)**

a) ☐ Vincent (2006)

b) ☐ Bytheway (1995)

c) ☐ Featherstone (1999)

4 *During the period of 1998–2001, what was the percentage of pensioners living in poverty?* **(3 points)**

a) ☐ 35 per cent

b) ☐ 18 per cent

c) ☐ 9 per cent

5 *Which age group are most likely to be victims of crime?* **(4 points)**

a) ☐ Young males

b) ☐ Pensioners

c) ☐ Young females

Possible 17 points

13–17 Well done! You are an age expert!

8–12 It's official: you are becoming a 'sociology star'!

4–7 Looks like you might be avoiding the more difficult questions – get back to reading that textbook!

0–3 Oh dear, you're not going to win any 'sociology student of the year' prizes!

Answers: 1.a, 2.c, 3.a, 4.b, 5.a

Theory identifier

The statements below reflect the viewpoints of one of the following theories: Marxism, functionalism, Weberianism or postmodernism. Identify which theory goes with which statement by writing in the space above the statement.

1 _____

This theory identifies a key process known as disengagement; this process concerns itself with the role old age plays within the social system. Those who are ageing seek to abandon some social roles, leaving them for the younger generation to pick up; this process is believed to maintain social order.

2 _____

This theory associates the loss of power and status with the ageing process. McKingsley (2001) supports this theory by arguing that old age and retirement can be construed as triggers for a loss of status. Without a strong market and work situation an individual's status is ultimately reduced.

3 _____

This theory believes that the increase in individual choice and the destruction of categories such as age in society has made age an increasingly fragmented and diverse social category.

4 _____

This theory applies the 'reserve army of labour' thesis to both ends of the working age spectrum. Both groups can meet the needs of an economy in times of boom and bust therefore both groups can be easily hired and fired.

Applying research studies task

The following is a list of some of the key concepts you may need to refer to when answering questions on age inequality. Fill in the spaces in the adjacent column with details of a sociologist/theorist and their research which could be used to illustrate each concept. The first one is done for you. Answers can be found at the back of the book.

Key concepts	Sociologist/research/theory
Individualisation	This concept has been applied to an individual's life trajectory – individual choice has made age an increasingly fragmented and diverse social category.
'Negatively privileged status groups' (age)	
'Young elderly'	
'Reserve army of labour' (age)	
Dual labour market (age)	

ExamCafé

Exploring social inequality and difference: age

Exam answer-based activity

The answer below is an example of a well-written response to a G674 age question. Your task is to match the examiner's comments listed at the bottom with the numbers listed in the body of the exam answer. You must match the lettered examiner comments with the numbered points. You can then check at the bottom of the page to see if you are correct. The purpose of this activity is to give you an awareness of the key points which are required to answer this question and of where the skills of AO1, AO2a and AO2b are being used.

Question 3 / 4 (a)
Outline the evidence that age inequalities exist in the contemporary UK. (20 marks)

Student answer

Age is one of the forms of social stratification; it can be defined chronologically: as you get older you reach different socially defined markers of age. For example, when you reach 16 years of age you can legally work full time and at 18 years of age you can officially vote. Age can also be defined by life stages: youth, middle age and old age; within each stage of our life span we acquire different roles and statuses. The first stage of the life course is the period of youth: this is described by functionalists as a period of transition from childhood to adulthood (Eisenstadt, 1956). **1** ☐

At different points in our lifetime we can be more vulnerable to inequality; one of the key areas for inequality to exist is in the workplace. The workplace can be an environment of exploitation, particularly at the polar opposite times of life stage. Marxists argue that both ends of the spectrum of age can be exploited by the capitalist economy; Marxists apply the 'reserve army of labour' theory to explain how this process takes place. Marxist supporters argue that those under 14 years are exploited through cheap labour by the informal economy of newspaper delivery, whereas those over 65 actively seek part-time employment after retirement, due to financial commitments. Oppenheim and Harker (1996) found that only 73 per cent of male employees received a company pension, with the figure as low as 68 per cent for women; this may explain why people continue to work after pensionable age. Marxists argue that both groups meet the needs of the economy, and can be easily hired and fired at will. **2** ☐

Furthermore, both the very old and the very young are more susceptible to the extremes of inequality in the form of poverty. McKingsley (2001) argues that there are two groups that can be considered as pensioners: the first are just past retirement age and engage in 'active ageing', the second he calls the 'oldest old' – this group is generally over 80 years of age and has limited status and power within society. Milne and Harding's (1999) study found that those over 85 years of age were more likely to be living alone with few savings and on the brink of poverty. In 2006 Giddens found that during the period of 1998-2001, 18 per cent of pensioners lived in poverty compared with only 7 per cent of the working population. Young children from low income and lone-parent households are also more likely to live in poverty. The Joseph Rowntree Foundation (1998) found that during the period of 1994-95, 75 per cent of lone parents and their children were in the poorest 40 per cent. For children living in poverty this has a detrimental effect on their ability to succeed in education. The National Children's Bureau (2003) reported that children from families living on state benefits were two thirds less likely to get at least 5 A*-C grades than those from more affluent backgrounds. **3** ☐

The middle life stage, known as middle age, can also be a period of inequality; the media is instrumental in marginalising the representation of this stage of life. Many consumer products that are marketed at this age group focus on the social desirability of youth: the advertisement of products such as the L'Oreal range of age-defying serums informally controls individuals. The cultural effects model of media effects can be applied to explain the effect that advertisement has on the middle aged; they are socialised through the media to believe that youth and beauty equal high status and success. **4** ☐

Pensioners are also marginalised by the media. Carrigan and Szmigin (2000) argue that the advertising industry either ignores older people or stereotypes them as being vulnerable and decrepit; the physical process of ageing is not seen as desirable but ugly.

Age inequality is evident at different stages of our life time. It would appear from the evidence stated that the two extreme stages of youth and old age are the periods of time in which we are more susceptible to inequality.

Examiner comments

a) Consideration made of more than one age group, with links into several studies on poverty and education. This part of the response would gain marks for AO1 and AO2a.

b) Good use of theory with links into supporting statistical data on workplace and pensions. This part of the response would gain marks for AO1 and AO2a.

c) Good link into the influence of the mass media, supported by reference to a media effects model. This part of the response would gain marks for AO1.

d) Concepts are defined and directly linked into theory. This part of the response would gain marks for AO1.

Now try your own

Now try to write answers to the questions below. It is a good idea to try writing these answers under timed conditions. You should spend approximately 20 minutes writing each answer.

◆ Outline the evidence supporting the view that age inequalities are most likely to happen during the period of old age. (20 marks)

◆ Outline the evidence that argues that the very young and the very old are most susceptible to age inequality. (20 marks)

Assess Marxist explanations of age inequalities. (40 marks)

Student answer

Age is one of the forms of stratification, alongside social class, gender and ethnicity; a person's age can determine their life chances. Laslett (1991) states that there are three ages of life, the last being a time of independence, free from the responsibilities of work and child rearing, a time when those over the age of 65 can engage in 'active ageing' (Waugh et al., 2008). However, Marxists would argue that during the first and the third ages of life an individual's age can be used by capitalists as a justification for paying the minimum wage. The Marxist idea of the 'reserve army of labour' can be applied to the notion of age inequalities in the workplace; they argue that those under 14 years are exploited through cheap labour by the informal economy of newspaper delivery, whereas those over 65 actively seek part-time employment after retirement, due to financial commitments. Marxists go on further to argue that the welfare state provision for the young and old in the form of child benefit and state pensions could be viewed as an attempt to make these age groups dependent on the state and that in fact the welfare state is part of the ideological state apparatus. Marxists argue that laws such as the official retirement age of 65 years benefit the capitalist economy. The official retirement age takes those over 65 out of the workplace, which in turn means that private companies can get in younger staff, who will have less skill and maybe less human capital, which will mean that private companies will be able to pay the younger staff less than their retired counterparts, thus limiting the strain on the private companies' economic resources. **1** ☐

However, functionalists would argue against the notion that the state forces those over 65 out of employment; they believe that a process of disengagement takes place. They state that individuals become aware of the fact that they are ageing and that it is the individuals themselves who 'actively seek to abandon certain social roles', i.e. being employees, and by leaving work they make way for the younger generation. This process helps to maintain social order as there is a value consensus that those of retirement age should make way for the younger generation. **2** ☐

Postmodernists Featherstone and Hepworth (1999) argue that in the contemporary UK individual life courses are becoming increasingly deconstructed and fragmented, meaning that due to the fact that more and more people are choosing to work past the official age of retirement in a bid to maintain their lifestyle and their achieved status, there are no clear patterns of age-related behaviour; therefore it is very difficult to apply the structural theories of Marxism and functionalism in an analysis of age inequality. **3** ☐

However, Marxists would argue that the state is instrumental in perpetuating workplace inequalities, particularly for those under the age of 21. The minimum wage for those aged 18-21 is £4.77 per hour and £3.53 for those between the ages of 16 and 18, while for apprentices under 19 years the minimum wage does not apply (HM Revenue and Customs, 2009). Private companies can make large profits from the 'surplus value' of those on the minimum wage. **4** ☐

Weberian theorists would argue that Marxist analysis is too reductionist and that age inequality goes beyond just economic factors. Weberian theory is more concerned with the loss of status and power that an individual experiences at different points of their life course. According to McKingsley (2001), old age can be a trigger for a loss of status and this is something that is cultural as well as economic. It is argued by Weberians that without a strong market and work situation an individual will inevitably lose status and power. Parkin's (1968) concept of 'negatively privileged status groups' can be applied to those in old age who have lost their position in the labour market and are considered either as 'too old to employ' or are being sidelined for younger, more upwardly mobile employees. However, postmodernists would argue that age-related status positions will vary due to the process of individualisation:

individual choice has fragmented age as a social category. Within the entertainment and sports industries there are many examples of how the ageing process has not affected the life chances and opportunities open to those aged over 65 years. Clint Eastwood, in 2004 and at the age of 74, won an Oscar for best director of the film *Million Dollar Baby*: it has become more possible for individuals not to be restricted by typical expectations of how older people should behave or think. **5** ☐

However, other forms of employment do not offer the same opportunities. According to the findings of the MORI survey of 2002, one in five workers from all age sectors stated that they had experienced age discrimination at work, with 30 per cent citing ageism as the cause (MORI, 2002).

There are many criticisms of the Marxist analysis of age, particularly that it is unconvincing in its account of age disadvantage in the contemporary UK (Waugh et al., 2009). Functionalism has been argued as the theory which is most applicable to the study of age inequality; however, it has been accused of homogenising age experience and failing to recognise how an individual's other social characteristics of gender, class or ethnicity, which intersect with age, can influence an individual's life chances. **6** ☐

Overall, considering the explanations put forth in this essay, it is apparent that not one single theory can explain the complexities of age inequality. The theories are in the process of being developed and although they cannot explain age inequalities in great detail, they are useful in helping us to understand how age inequalities take place.

Examiner comments

a) Good use of alternative theory, stating clearly that the individual is consciously aware of the need for them to step out of the labour market. This response would gain marks for AO1.

b) Good direct evaluation of structural theories by the use of another theory. This part of the response would gain marks for AO1 and AO2b.

c) Good evaluation of Marxist and functionalist theory, highlighting the overall limitations of both theories. This part of the response would gain marks for AO2b.

d) Good use of the skills of AO1 and AO2a in the interpretation of Marxist theory.

e) Interesting point made about the minimum wage; however, 'surplus value' could be explained in greater detail. This part of the response would gain marks for AO1 and AO2a.

f) Good use of another theory. The postmodern theory is illustrated well with the reference to the entertainment industry. This part of the response would gain marks for all three skills.

Now try your own

Now try to write answers to the questions below. It is a good idea to try writing these answers under timed conditions. You should spend 45 minutes writing each answer.

◆ Assess Weberian explanations of age inequalities. (40 marks)

◆ Assess the view that ethnic inequalities no longer exist in the contemporary UK. (40 marks)

Research methods

Revision checklist

You are at stage one of the revision process; the list below outlines all the topics and sub-topics which you need to cover in your revision. Take time now to make sure you have everything you need to revise this part of the course. The points referred to below can all be found in the core textbook. Your teacher(s) may also have taught you other sociological research studies in which case you should also revise these. Tick off the areas once you have revised them and track your progress through the topics.

Key concepts
All the concepts you need to know are listed on the 'Key concepts' activity pages. Please check that you are able to define all these concepts and understand how they are applied to sociological research.

Methodological issues and concerns
You should have an understanding of the following theoretical perspectives, the research methods they favour, the concepts associated with them, and be able to evaluate them.

- Positivist ☐
- Interpretivist ☐
- Realist ☐
- Feminist ☐

Key concepts

This recap activity will ensure that you go over those all-important key concepts.
Complete the key concept chart by writing a definition of the concept. Refer to
your core textbook or your classroom notes.

Key concepts	Definitions
Quantitative	
Qualitative	
Positivism	
Interpretivism	
Validity	
Reliability	
Representativeness	
Generalisability	
Primary research	
Secondary research	
Operationalisation	
Methodological pluralism	
Triangulation	
Ethics	
Longitudinal studies	
Case studies	

Key concepts	Definitions
Pilot studies	
Value freedom	
Objectivity	
Subjectivity	
Respondent validation	
Researcher imposition	
Reflexivity	
Target population	
Access	
Gatekeeper	
Random sampling	
Stratified sampling	
Quota sampling	
Snowball sampling	
Purposeful/purposive sampling	

Mix and match

The purpose of this exercise is to test your knowledge of the research methods process, including quantitative and qualitative methods. You will need to match the explanation of the research/theory with the name of the sociologist/concept. Each sociologist/concept is numbered and the explanation of the research/theory is lettered. Identify the correct explanations by writing the correct letters in the blank boxes provided. Then check at the bottom of the next page to see if you have matched them correctly.

Sociologist/concept

1 Questionnaires ☐

2 Statistical data ☐

3 Ethnography ☐

4 Observation ☐

5 Semi-structured interviews ☐

6 Durkheim ☐

7 Operationalisation ☐

Research/theory/definition

A
This term can be applied to the process of breaking down a research question, aim or hypothesis into something that can be measured.

B
This theorist has been described as a positivist. He believed that sociological research should study social facts, which he argued are things which are external to social actors.

C
This term is used by interpretivists who use the term to explain the use of methods which allow the researcher to place themselves in the position of those being studied.

D
This methodology believes that sociological research can follow the logic and methods of the natural sciences; it distinguishes between open and closed systems of science.

E
This sociologist argued that feminist methodology is based around the common features of using the research process and methods with the aim of bringing about social change. Feminist methodology argues that the researcher should not be seen as a separate 'other' and they stress the need for a rapport to be developed between the researcher and the participants.

F
This term is concerned with the extent to which a researcher can achieve objectivity.

G
This is where participants are used to check the data gathered during the study. Participants may be asked to comment on their own interview transcript, to ensure they are a valid interpretation of what took place during the collection of the data.

(continued)

Sociologist/concept

8 *Verstehen*	☐

9 Qualitative data-collection methods	☐

10 'Respondent validation'	☐

11 Quantitative data-collection methods	☐

12 Structured interviews	☐

13 Realist	☐

14 'Value freedom'	☐

15 Reinhartz (1992)	☐

Research/theory/definition

H
This method of data collection is favoured by positivists. Such forms of data collection are useful in creating numerical data which can be easily replicated when dealing with large sample sizes and data sets.

I
An advantage of this method type is that it allows for standardised responses to standardised questions – all respondents are faced with the same questions in the same order and format.

J
A disadvantage of this method type is the potential for the researcher to influence the participants. Participants can be affected by the researcher's body language and tone of voice, which could affect the overall validity of the data collected.

K
This research method could also be considered quantitative due to the flexible nature of the method, which allows for the collection of quantitative data to be possible.

L
This is a secondary method of data which is considered as being reliable due to the fact that the data generated can be checked year on year.

M
This method of data collection is favoured by interpretivists and many feminists. Such methods of data collection create rich, valid and textual data.

N
This qualitative method includes the following types; participant/non-participant and structured and non-structured. This method allows the researcher to see the individuals they are studying in their natural environment.

O
This is a disadvantage of this method: insider knowledge/status may be required for access and can lead to problems in gaining objective data.

Answers: 1.I, 2.L, 3.O, 4.N, 5.K, 6.B, 7.A, 8.C, 9.M, 10.G, 11.H, 12.J, 13.D, 14.F, 15.E

Check your knowledge quick fire quiz

This multiple choice quiz will test your knowledge on the topic of research methods. Each question will be worth a number of points; the points are indicated at the end of the question. The more points a question is worth, the more difficult it is: the top mark questions reflect whether you have read your core textbook thoroughly. Once you have ticked the answer you believe to be correct, add up your score to reveal whether you are a research methods expert!

1 *This concept is described as a form of self-evaluation, where the researcher is consciously aware of the effect they could be having on the research participants and research data. Which of the following is the concept described above?* **(3 points)**

a) ☐ Reflexivity

b) ☐ Flexibility

c) ☐ Subjectivity

2 *This method type is part primary/part secondary and has been used by sociologists such as Van Dijk (1991) in the study of ethnic representation in the media. What is the method called?* **(4 points)**

a) ☐ Data analysis

b) ☐ Content analysis

c) ☐ Semiotic analysis

3 *Which type of observation could be considered as the most unethical?* **(3 points)**

a) ☐ Covert participant observation

b) ☐ Overt participant observation

c) ☐ Covert non-participant observation

4 *Which of the following interview types allows for a number of respondents to share beliefs, attitudes and experiences at the same time?* **(3 points)**

a) ☐ Semi-structured interview

b) ☐ Structured interview

c) ☐ Focus group interview

5 *Which of the following forms of secondary data carries with it the disadvantage of the data's creditability and authenticity being questioned?* **(4 points)**

a) ☐ Personal documents

b) ☐ Statistical data

c) ☐ Existing sociological research

6 *Identify the approach used in mixed methods which allows the researcher to build up a more complete and accurate account of what they are researching.* **(3 points)**

a) ☐ Triangulation

b) ☐ Methodological pluralism

c) ☐ Content analysis

7 *Which type of study is carried out over a period of time, with the intent of noting the process of change over time?* **(3 points)**

a) ☐ Longitudinal study

b) ☐ Long period of time study

c) ☐ Long-term study

8 *Identify the name of a study which is also known as a preliminary study?* **(3 points)**

a) ☐ Small sample study

b) ☐ Pilot study

c) ☐ Pre-study

9 *Which of the following is not an official sample frame?* **(4 points)**

a) ☐ School register

b) ☐ Post-code address file

c) ☐ Address book

10 *Which of the following is not an ethical concern?* **(3 points)**

a) ☐ Informed consent

b) ☐ Confidentiality

c) ☐ Operationalisation

Possible 33 points

22–33 Well done! You are a research methods expert!

15–21 It's official: you are becoming a 'sociology star'

9–14 Looks like you might be avoiding the more difficult questions – get back to reading that textbook!

0–8 Oh dear, you're not going to win any 'sociology student of the year' prizes!

Answers: 1.a, 2.b, 3.a, 4.c, 5.a, 6.b, 7.a, 8.b, 9.c, 10.c

ExamCafé

Exploring social inequality and difference: research methods

Questions one and two

Questions one and two are the compulsory elements of the G674 paper. Question one will require you to refer to the source material below; you can also refer to the source material for question two if the material is applicable. On pages 108–109 are examples of a well-written question one answer and a well-written question two answer.

Young people today face complex decisions about their future lives, particularly as they leave compulsory education and begin the transition into adulthood. Research by Midgley and Bradshaw entitled 'Should I stay or should I go?' explores the experiences of 16–19-year-olds in rural areas as they leave compulsory education. It focuses on the options available to them as they move from education, to training and employment, and sometimes back again.

The methodology starts from the belief that the most valuable and powerful insights into the lives of young people are offered by researching the views of young people themselves. The research is located within interpretivism. The research participants were all aged 16–19 and were from four different parts of rural England. In each area focus groups were held with the following groups of young people:

- Not in employment, education or training (females, NEET*)
- Not in employment, education or training (males, NEET*)
- In employment (females/males together)
- In education and training (females/males together)

The focus groups were conducted during March 2006, and each group had between three and six participants drawn exclusively from one of the groups stated above. Males and females who were not in employment, education or training were placed in separate focus groups as this allowed specific gendered impacts and influences to be explored. The young people were encouraged to talk about their experiences and aspirations as they left compulsory education. The majority of participants had lived in the same rural area all of their lives, and were from working-class backgrounds. In addition to this 24 semi-structured interviews were also conducted with workers in organisations that have contact with young people in rural areas.

The research found that young people in rural areas do not have access to the education and training opportunities they need and want, and to which they are entitled. One 16-year-old female NEET said, 'You go into a job centre and it's really hard. Especially being only 16 with no qualifications. If you don't need qualifications, like working in a shop, then they want experience, which you don't have if you are 16.' A 17-year-old male NEET said, 'I am now planning to do plumbing, but you need an apprenticeship and it's hard to find one around here.'

Large numbers of the young people in this research felt they had to 'get out' of the rural area they lived in in order to 'get on'. This has serious consequences for the long-term future of rural areas.

Adapted from 'Should I Stay or Should I Go? Rural youth transitions', by Jane Midgley and Ruth Bradshaw, Institute for Public Policy Research (IPPR), 2006.

*NEET is an acronym for those not in employment, education or training

Question one
Using the item and your knowledge outline and explain how focus groups may be used in sociological research. (15 marks)

Student answer

Highly valid data can be achieved through observing and recording the social interactions between participants during focus-group discussion. Midgley and Bradshaw used the qualitative method of focus groups in their 2006 study into young people and the options open to them once they left compulsory education in rural districts. Focus groups are a very valid method when studying young people; participants within the group could be encouraged to take part as they may feel supported by others within the group who have similar experiences. This will allow the focus-group facilitator to obtain in-depth valid data, which may have not have been discovered during a one-to-one interview. Midgley and Bradshaw wanted to optimise the validity of their data by ensuring that within the four focus groups, participants were grouped together based on their social characteristics (male/female) and their post-education experiences. If they were not in employment, education and training (NEETS) they were placed in two separate gendered groups, as Midgley and Bradshaw believed the dynamics of these groups were important in drawing out specific gendered impacts, influences and experiences. In separating these two groups from the other two groups (one included those in employment and the other those in training and education) they helped to prevent the problem of socially desirable responses. Participants from the NEET group, if they had been mixed with the non-NEET groups, may have felt intimidated and may even have felt that they may be judged by the non-NEETs. This could have resulted in socially desirable responses, reducing the validity of the study, or the participants may have withdrawn from the discussion altogether, reducing the representativeness.

Question two
Outline and assess the claim made by some sociologists that the most valuable and powerful insights into the lives of young people are offered by researching the views of young people themselves. (25 marks)

Student answer

Interpretivists believe that human beings are diverse and that in order for social researchers to understand social reality, researchers need to actively engage with participants. Focus groups are part of the interpretative school of research methodology, alongside qualitative interviews and observations. Sociologists who favour such methods support the view that in order to understand the meanings that young people attach to their experiences and behaviour, it is necessary for the researcher to develop a sense of verstehen with the young participants. Midgley and Bradshaw in their 2006 study on young people argued that the most 'powerful insights' come from the young people themselves; therefore, methods need to be used which empower young people and make them feel comfortable enough to provide data that is rich in detail. This is why Midgley and Bradshaw opted for the qualitative method of focus groups, as they believed that being placed in groups where participants had similar experiences would empower them to feel supported and would help them to open up, thus providing the focus-group facilitator with highly valid data. However, those that favour a more positivist methodological framework would argue that due to the lack of standardisation in the focus-group method, it would be almost impossible to replicate the research, therefore preventing future researchers from testing the reliability of the data gathered. Furthermore, it could be argued that due to group dynamics, the validity of such a method could be questionable as participants may provide socially desirable answers, even if they have similar experiences to the rest of the group members. Also, there may be personality differences which may prevent quieter members of the group from participating; therefore, the data gathered may not be representative of all members of the focus group. Moreover, ethically it could be argued that it would be more suitable to use quantitative methods such as questionnaires and structured interviews when seeking the opinions of young people, as common qualitative methods such as focus groups and unstructured interviews may stir up emotions and cause some distress to the young people. The British Sociological Association (BSA) states that due care and attention needs to be paid to particularly vulnerable groups, such as young people, in the carrying out of sociological research and that no unnecessary physical or psychological harm should come to them.

However, if researchers are to gather valid data on experiences, then it is necessary and justifiable to use qualitative methods of research: the only way to truly gain the views of young people is to put them in a situation in which they will feel comfortable enough to provide valid responses. Furthermore, it may be useful for researchers to use a mixed-methods approach by triangulating the methods. Structured interviews or questionnaires could be used to cross-check the validity of the data gathered from qualitative methods such as focus groups.

Conclusion

Top ten tips for the exam

1 Ensure that your class notes are in order; it might be helpful to use dividers to separate your notes on each unit.

2 It is a good idea to keep testing yourself to see what you can remember and to then make a note of those points that you are struggling to remember. You can then go over them and test yourself again.

3 Try out a range of revision techniques to see which is most effective for you (see the introduction of this book for ideas on how to effectively revise).

4 Make sure you are familiar with the exam paper layout and that you carefully read not only the assessment questions but the instructions as well. This will ensure that your response includes everything that it should.

5 Take note of the total marks for each part of the question; this will help you to decide on how long you should spend on each part of the overall question.

6 Do plenty of practice exam questions. This is useful not only in terms of checking your knowledge, but it will also allow you to check your timing. You must ensure that you can write a full response in the time allocated.

7 If you are concerned that you may forget information when you get into the exam, then it is a good idea to write any information down, e.g. sociologists names, concepts, etc., as soon as you are given permission to write in the exam, before you read the question.

8 Make sure that you plan your answer before you write it, particularly for those questions which are worth the greatest amount of marks.

9 Once you have completed your answers, it is worth taking the time to read over them again, to see if you can develop them further and to check for any errors or points that you may have missed.

10 Once you have finished the exam and have left the exam venue, try not to think about the answers you have given. Be confident that if you have put in the hard work during your AS and A2 years, and you have revised effectively by following the tips and activities in this book, then you should be successful.

Answers

Please note, the page references below refer to where you can find the study (or a description of the concept) in the accompanying textbook – *OCR Sociology A2* by Waugh et al.

Crime and deviance: applying research studies task

Anomie	Durkheim (1893) page 13
Meritocracy	Merton (1938) page 13
Cultural deprivation	New right page 15
Material deprivation	Marxism page 19
Chivalry thesis	Pollack (1950) page 26
Corporate crime	Marxists page 20
Folk devils	Cohen page 35
Broken windows	New right page 38

Education: applying research studies task

Role allocation	Davis and Moore (1945) page 57
Cultural capital	Bourdieu (1973) page 59
Self-fulfilling prophecy	Rosenthal and Jacobsen (1968) page 62
Immediate gratification	Sugarman (1970) page 66
Elaborated and restricted language codes	Bernstein (1961) page 67
Material deprivation	Smith and Noble (1995) page 69
Anti-school subcultures	Willis (1977) page 74
Bedroom culture	Mitsos and Browne (1998) page 72
Institutional racism	Coard page 77
Cheap labour	Davies and Biesta (2007) page 82
Knowledge economy	Ball (2008) page 84
Personalisation	New Labour page 85
EMA	Machin and Vignoles (2006) page 85

Mass media: applying research studies task

Repressive state apparatus (RSA)	Althusser (1977) page 130
Moral panic	Cohen (1972) page 133
Hyper-reality	Baudrillard (1988) page 114
News values	Galtung and Ruge (1965) page 106
'Hierarchy of credibility'	Marshall (1998) page 108
News diary	Schlesinger (1987) page 108
Global village	McLuhan and Fiore (1971) page 114
'Malestream'	Radical feminists page 123
Hypodermic syringe model	Packard (1957) page 126
Catharsis	Feshbach and Singer (1971) page 127
Two-step flow model	Katz and Lazarsfeld (1955) page 127
Uses and gratification model	McQuail (1972) page 128
'Folk devils'	Cohen (1972) page 133
Hegemony	Neo-Marxism page 103

Power and politics: applying research studies task

Resource mobilisation theory (RMT)	Social movement *page 151*
Risk society	Beck (1992) *page 159*
Global imperialism	An element of Americanisation *page 159*
McJobs	Ritzer (1996) *page 159*
Culture jamming	Subverting a company's adverts as a form of political action *page 160*
Eco-warriors	Allen (2000) *page 173*
Cyber-balkanisation	Putnam (2000) *page 146*
Social movement organisations (SMOs)	Social movements with some formal organisation *pages 151–152*
Meritocracies	Liberalism *page 165*

Class: applying research studies task

Meritocracy	Davis and Moore (1945) *page 195*
Deskilling	Braverman (1974) *page 204*
Ideological state apparatus	Althusser (1977) *page 187*
Contradictory class location	Wright (1997) *page 196*
Embourgeoisement	Goldthorpe (1968) *page 203*
Cultural reproduction	Marxists *page 198*
Proletarianisation	Braverman (1974) *page 204*
Underclass	Runciman (1990), Roberts (1997), Murray (1994) *page 205*

Gender: applying research studies task

Reserve army of labour	Beechey (1976) *page 214*
Dual systems theory	Hartmann (1981) *page 216*
Preference theory	Hakim (2000) *page 218*
Patriarchy	Firestone (1971), Millett (1971) *page 217*
Positive discrimination	Friedan (1963) *page 215*
Expressive roles	Parsons (1955) *page 214*
Instrumental roles	Parsons (1955) *page 214*

Ethnicity: applying research studies task

'Negatively privileged status groups'	Parkin (1968) *page 225*
'American negro'	Parsons (1966) *page 224*
'Divide-and-rule tactic'	Cox (1948) *page 224*
Intentional racism	Overt and conscious racism *pages 220–221*

Age: applying research studies task

'Negatively privileged status groups' (age)	Parkin (1968) *pages 230–231*
'Young elderly'	Milne and Harding (1999) *page 228*
'Reserve army of labour' (age)	Marxism *page 230*
Dual labour market (age)	Weberian theory *page 231*

Answers